S. Hrg. 113–377

FRAUD AND ABUSE IN ARMY RECRUITING CONTRACTS

HEARING

BEFORE THE

SUBCOMMITTEE ON FINANCIAL AND CONTRACTING OVERSIGHT

OF THE

COMMITTEE ON HOMELAND SECURITY AND GOVERNMENTAL AFFAIRS UNITED STATES SENATE

ONE HUNDRED THIRTEENTH CONGRESS

SECOND SESSION

FEBRUARY 4, 2014

Available via the World Wide Web: http://www.fdsys.gov

Printed for the use of the Committee on Homeland Security and Governmental Affairs

U.S. GOVERNMENT PRINTING OFFICE

88–274 PDF   WASHINGTON : 2014

For sale by the Superintendent of Documents, U.S. Government Printing Office
Internet: bookstore.gpo.gov   Phone: toll free (866) 512–1800; DC area (202) 512–1800
Fax: (202) 512–2104   Mail: Stop IDCC, Washington, DC 20402–0001

CONTENTS

FRAUD AND ABUSE IN ARMY RECRUITING CONTRACTS

TUESDAY, FEBRUARY 4, 2014

U.S. SENATE,
SUBCOMMITTEE ON FINANCIAL AND CONTRACTING OVERSIGHT
OF THE COMMITTEE ON HOMELAND SECURITY
AND GOVERNMENTAL AFFAIRS,
Washington, DC.

The Subcommittee met, pursuant to notice, at 10:02 a.m., in room SD–342, Dirksen Senate Office Building, Hon. Claire McCaskill, Chairman of the Subcommittee, presiding.

Present: Senators McCaskill, Johnson, and Ayotte.

OPENING STATEMENT OF SENATOR MCCASKILL

Senator MCCASKILL. Welcome, everyone. I know that my colleague has a time crunch this morning and so I am going to try to begin right away so we can hopefully get time for both of us to have some questions before he has to go. Let me begin with a very brief opening statement.

This hearing will now come to order.

The Recruiting Assistance Program (RAP) was born in 2005 when the Army National Guard (ARNG) was struggling to meet its recruitment numbers due to the wars in Afghanistan and Iraq. The National Guard's Recruiting Assistance Program (G–RAP), would provide incentives to National Guard soldiers and civilians to act as informal recruiters, or recruiting assistants (RA). These recruiting assistants would receive a payment between $2,000 and $7,500 for every new recruit. The contract was run out of the Army National Guard's Strength Maintenance Division (ASM), and administered by a contractor, Docupak. The recruiting assistants were hired by Docupak as subcontractors. After the program was put in place, the National Guard began to meet its recruiting goals and the Active Army and Army Reserve began their own similar programs.

In 2007, however, Docupak discovered instances of potential fraud, which it referred to the Army. Four years later, after suspecting a pattern of fraud, the Army requested a program-wide audit, and what the audit found was astounding—thousands of National Guard and Army Reserve participants who are associated with payments that are at high or medium risk for fraud, with an estimated total amount of $29 million paid fraudulently. This criminal fraud investigation is one of the largest that the Army has ever conducted, both in terms of sheer volume of fraud and the number of participants.

(1)

Although recruiters were prohibited from participating in the RAP program because recruiting was already part of their job duties, investigators found that potentially over 1,200 recruiters fraudulently obtained payments. For example, in Texas, a former member of the National Guard was sentenced to 4 years and 9 months in prison for leading a conspiracy to obtain $244,000 in fraudulent recruiting bonuses. He did this by providing kickbacks to National Guard recruiters in return for the names and Social Security numbers of recruits who had, in fact, already been recruited.

The fraud was not limited to service members. Because anyone could sign up to be a recruiting assistant, there are also cases of people unaffiliated with the Army stealing names and Social Security numbers of potential recruits and receiving referral payments that they were not entitled to.

Even one case of fraud would have been too many. Instead, we now know that thousands of service members, their families and friends may have participated in schemes to defraud the government they served and the taxpayers. Worst of all, this program has the potential to become a stain on thousands of recruiters and National Guard members who do their jobs so well and so honorably.

And when I looked into how this could have happened, the story just got worse. According to the auditors, the National Guard made mistake after mistake in designing and implementing the program that left it vulnerable to exactly the kind of fraud that occurred. In addition, Army auditors found that the contracts failed to comply with government contracting rules, including basic requirements to conduct the kind of minimal oversight that could have detected and prevented some of this fraud.

And as if all that was not bad enough, the Army has determined in its investigation that the entire program was illegal from the beginning. The payments did not fall in a permissible category of bonus payments authorized by law. The program also exceeded the limits that Congress had placed on legal bonuses the Army could pay to encourage the referral of new recruits. As a result, the Army concluded that all of the money spent on the program, all $386 million of it, was illegal.

I cannot begin to express how disappointed and angry I am to hear of such carelessness with taxpayer dollars. I appreciate that recruiting is key to maintaining our military strength and key to making sure that we have the skills that our military needs, particularly in wartime. But we have to make sure that we are going about it the right way.

Congress and the American public have entrusted the Army with taxpayer dollars and with upholding standards of integrity. We cannot have programs fly in the face of law and good government practice simply to meet recruiting numbers, no matter how desperate the situation.

To its credit, the Army's leadership immediately suspended the program back in 2012 when the auditors began to expose these massive problems, and they began a variety of investigations to determine how this could happen and who was responsible. Some of those investigations are still ongoing and I look forward to learning the results when they are completed.

However, I am disappointed that it took a small story in the Washington Post in 2012 for this Subcommittee to even have an inkling about problems with this large contract, and that it took almost 2 years and our repeated insistence for the Army to inform the Subcommittee that the problems that the Post reported were just the tip of the iceberg. Since then, the Army has cooperated fully with our requests and I thank them for that.

Today, I want to spend some time delving into exactly what went wrong in the design and management of this program and how so many mistakes were made. I also want to discuss what the Army is doing to hold all the individuals involved accountable. I will also ask questions about what concrete steps the Army has taken to address all the deficiencies uncovered so far.

I thank you all for being here today and I look forward to your testimony. Senator Johnson.

OPENING STATEMENT OF SENATOR JOHNSON

Senator JOHNSON. Thank you, Madam Chairman, and let me apologize for having to leave at about 10:25. I also want to thank you for holding this hearing and your pursuit of this particular issue in terms of oversight. I think it is definitely an important issue. I want to thank the witnesses who have taken time to meet with me in my office and also provide me some of the information, because this can be pretty detailed and pretty complex, exactly what happened here.

From my standpoint, I think you did a pretty good job laying out the issues, laying out what the problem was. I basically have three questions. Did the National Guard have the legal authority to do what it did? I think that is still certainly a question in my mind. It sounded like they sought legal counsel. I think the question is whether there was undue pressure put to get basically those legal opinions to allow them to do this. I think that is a question we have to certainly ask.

Has there been accountability and will there be accountability? Will there be accountability for those individuals that basically took the authority to institute this program, which obviously went awry? And then, do we have proper corrective action so this does not happen in the future? To me, those are the three big questions.

I think I am heartened by the fact, and I think you would probably agree with this, that the Army did, once they became aware of it, immediately suspend the program. I think the investigation that is going on now is serious. I think that there are criminal charges being filed and pursued, and I think that has to be the case.

So, from my standpoint, the program has been ended. I think this is very appropriate in terms of oversight. I think the fact that you have pushed this oversight hearing is certainly helping move this process along.

And, again, I just want to thank you. I wish I could stay longer, because this is an important issue.

Senator MCCASKILL. Thank you.

Senator JOHNSON. Thank you.

Senator MCCASKILL. I want to introduce our witnesses. Lieutenant General William Grisoli is Director of the Army Staff at the

Department of the Army Headquarters, a position he has held since July 2013. In this capacity, he is responsible for ensuring the effective integration and coordination of Army policy, positions, and procedures across the functional areas of Army responsibility. General Grisoli previously served as Director of the Army Office of Business Transformation within the Office of the Under Secretary of the Army.

Major General David Quantock is the Provost Marshal of the Army and Commanding General, United States Army Criminal Investigation Command (CID) and Army Corrections Command. He serves as the Army's top law enforcement official, with responsibility for investigations and incarcerations of Army personnel. General Quantock previously served as Commanding General of the U.S. Army Maneuvers Support Center of Excellence in the most excellent Fort Leonard Wood in Missouri.

Joseph Bentz is the Principal Deputy Auditor General with the U.S. Army Audit Agency (AAA), with responsibility for developing and overseeing the execution of the Army's internal audit plan and coordinating with other accountability organizations within the Federal Government. Prior to becoming Principal Deputy Auditor General, Mr. Bentz served as Deputy Auditor General for Acquisition, Logistics, and Technology Audits (ALT). So, you went from the Logistics Civil Augmentation Program (LOGCAP) to recruiting fraud.

OK. I want to thank you all for being here. It is the custom of this Committee for you to stand and take the oath.

Do you swear that the testimony that you are about to give will be the truth, the whole truth, and nothing but the truth, so help you, God?

General GRISOLI. I do.

General QUANTOCK. I do.

Mr. BENTZ. I do.

Senator MCCASKILL. Thank you very much.

And, we will begin with you, Major General Quantock.

General QUANTOCK. I think the opening statement will be with General Grisoli.

Senator MCCASKILL. Oh, great. OK.

TESTIMONY OF LIEUTENANT GENERAL WILLIAM T. GRISOLI,[1] DIRECTOR OF THE ARMY STAFF, U.S. ARMY; ACCOMPANIED BY MAJOR GENERAL DAVID E. QUANTOCK, PROVOST MARSHAL GENERAL OF THE ARMY, AND COMMANDING GENERAL, U.S. ARMY CRIMINAL INVESTIGATION COMMAND AND ARMY CORRECTIONS COMMAND; AND JOSEPH P. BENTZ, PRINCIPAL DEPUTY AUDITOR GENERAL, U.S. ARMY AUDIT AGENCY

General GRISOLI. Good morning, Chairman McCaskill and Ranking Member Johnson. Thank you for the opportunity to discuss the Recruiting Assistance Program and the Army's comprehensive efforts to detect, analyze, and investigate allegations of fraud and mismanagement.

---

[1] The prepared statement of Mr. Grisoli appears in the Appendix on page 41.

Before I discuss the particulars of the Recruiting Assistance Program, I want you to know that the accusations of fraud, mismanagement, and other potentially criminal activities surrounding this program are as disturbing to us as I know they are to you. You have my commitment that we will do whatever it takes to put this right, and you will hear today we have already done much, but there is more to be done. We will also punish those who have broken the law and recoup resources where we can.

The Recruiting Assistance Program was created in 2005 to bolster Army National Guard recruiting efforts during a period of increased demand coupled with the difficult recruiting market. RAP provided payments to recruiting assistants for each potential enlistee that enlisted and entered basic training. This effort was coordinated by a contractor, Docupak. All components of the Army implemented a form of RAP for various periods of time: The Army National Guard from 2005 to 2012; the Army Reserve from 2007 to 2012; and the active duty from 2008 to 2009. The total program was approximately $459 million.

In 2007, Docupak alerted the United States Army Criminal Investigation Command to possible fraud in the Recruiting Assistance Program. CID initiated several potential fraud case reviews, and in 2011 requested the U.S. Army Audit Agency begin a fraud risk assessment of the program. Upon learning of the preliminary results, in February 2012, the Secretary of the Army immediately canceled the Recruiting Assistance Program and directed the recovery of the remaining unexecuted RAP funds. He also issued a comprehensive directive to determine ultimate responsibility and accountability for the failures in the RAP program and to initiate appropriate corrective action. The Army created a task force to comprehensively and thoroughly review the scope, contracting organizational structural, contracting procedures, possible misuse of Army funds, and potential criminal activity.

In September 2013, I updated the Secretary of the Army on specific actions the Army had taken to determine ultimate responsibility and accountability for the failures in RAP and the corrective actions instituted. The Secretary of the Army subsequently signed another directive focused on additional corrective actions to ensure individual and organizational responsibility and accountability.

Currently, the Assistant Secretary of the Army (ASA) for Acquisition, Logistics, and Technology is reviewing the National Guard Bureau (NGB) and the Mission Installation Contracting Command Corrective Action Plans in response to their program management reviews, which found that there had been a general breakdown in sound business practices.

As indicated in my written testimony and by documents previously provided to the Subcommittee, corrective actions and investigations are still ongoing and with completion dates ranging from Spring 2014 to the end of 2016. You have my assurances we will continue to keep you informed as these investigations proceed.

In summary, the scope of the Recruiting Assistance Program investigations is complex and far-reaching. The Army has taken aggressive and comprehensive steps leading to corrective actions to prevent future occurrences and is committed to working with Congress as we move forward in this matter. Your focus helps us focus our oversight. The Army will also identify and take action against individuals who should be held accountable. I am confident the end result will be substantially improved recruiting and contracting processes in the National Guard Bureau and the entire United States Army.

Chairman McCaskill, Ranking Member Johnson, thank you for the time and interest in this matter. I look forward to your questions.

Senator McCaskill. Thank you so much.

I will just ask a couple of questions so there will still be some time left for you to ask questions before we leave.

Senator Johnson. OK.

Senator McCaskill. Let me get a sense of why it took 4 years from the time that Docupak gave you some indication that there was a problem? Can you lay out for us in a way that would make me feel more comfortable why it took until 2011 for the audit to be called for?

General Quantock. Chairman McCaskill, I can take a shot at that question.

Senator McCaskill. OK.

General Quantock. If you look at how the case came to everybody's attention, first of all, there were only two cases in 2007 that our CID investigation—that came through a fraud hotline that was——

Senator McCaskill. OK.

General Quantock [continuing]. Directed. So, understand that over this period of time, CID investigated over 43,000 felony criminal investigations.

Senator McCaskill. Right.

General Quantock. So, two cases in 2007 would not have raised.

And then in 2008, there were five cases.

Senator McCaskill. OK.

General Quantock. And then, of course, again, that would not send a signal, either. And then two more cases in 2009.

It was not until 2010 when we had 10 cases in 1 year that one of our Huntsville agents in Huntsville, Alabama, realized there is something that could be misconstrued or cause some kind of systematic concern. So, they raised it to us. We took a hard look at it. That is when we, basically, went over to AAA and said, can you take a hard look at this? There looks to be some systematic failures in this program. Could you do a deep dive on this program and see if there is anything that we need to be concerned about, other than the 19 cases that we are doing.

In addition to that, Docupak came to us in 2010, because they got the same 10 cases we did, and they also made us aware that they are seeing some irregularities, as well. So, it was a combination of Docupak, our agents at the Huntsville, Alabama, office, that really brought this to light, and that is when we transferred it over to AAA to take a hard look across the entire program.

Senator McCaskill. Well, make sure you convey to that investigator, that law enforcement professional in Huntsville, our appreciation that he raised the flag in 2010.

So, basically, what you are saying, General, is that up until 2010, these appeared to be isolated incidents as opposed to a pattern and a systemic fraud.

General QUANTOCK. Yes, ma'am. I have 150 fraud investigators, civilians, and we look at dozens of fraud investigations. So, this was just another one of those kind of dots on a map that cross the entire United States. Not only that, the 19 cases were, again, across the United States. So, there was really nothing that just jumped to our attention that would have directed us——

Senator MCCASKILL. OK.

General QUANTOCK [continuing]. That we have a major problem here.

Senator MCCASKILL. General Grisoli, one of the things—and I will get to questions for the auditor after Senator Johnson has a chance to question—but one of the things I am worried about is holding people accountable, and this is maybe a question for both you and General Quantock. I know that 2 years ago, we identified 1,200 recruiters and over 2,000 recruiting assistants. I know we are looking at a statute of limitations.

I am really concerned that there are going to be people that wear our uniform that are going to beat this by virtue of the statute of limitations, or they are only going to get "titled," and are not going to lose benefits, and will be allowed to retire and go their way. These are criminals who have dishonored the uniform that we are all so proud of, and I would like you to address briefly, if you would, what we need to be doing statutorily, whether that is lengthening the statute of limitations or making sure that there is some kind of procedure internally that you lose your benefits. I do not want to mess with anybody's benefits who served our country honorably, but if you have served dishonorably, I think you deserve more than the word "titled" in your file.

General GRISOLI. Madam Chairman, we have the same concern you have on this particular issue, and as we prioritize our efforts, we try to prioritize the ones of greater risk as falling into that category of where the statute of limitations.

As far as looking at some assistance from Congress, we are OK now, but I think we may have to come back and ask for some assistance, but we will let you know as we work with you through these problem sets and we address the highest priority first and the ones that are closest to the statutory limits. We will work through that and communicate with your staff.

Senator MCCASKILL. It is going to break my heart if there are a lot of people who get away with this, on behalf of all the amazingly brave and courageous people who step across the line. It is just going to break my heart, and we have to figure out a way to hold every single one of them accountable, if nothing else, just for the benefit of all those, the vast majority, that serve so well.

General GRISOLI. Madam Chairman, I would——

General QUANTOCK. I would agree. Go ahead, sir.

General GRISOLI. Madam Chairman, I would just say that this was one of our major points about prioritizing these cases was based on age of the case, so we could get after and do exactly that.

The other thing was going through—basically, we have 100,000 individuals that could be held accountable and trying to figure out the high-and the medium-and the low-risk, so we did not waste our time on the low-risk cases and we went after the high-and the medium-risk, and also the biggest dollar cost that was lost.

All of those things sort of were our focus, so we could really focus in. And that is why, today, we have 104 cases adjudicated, 16 individuals already in confinement, and we, again, continue to go after this very aggressively across the entire CID force.

Senator MCCASKILL. Great. Senator Johnson.

Senator JOHNSON. Thank you, Madam Chairman.

Let me just start out, because we discussed the history a little bit of recruiting bonuses, does anybody think just per se recruiting bonuses are a bad idea?

General GRISOLI. No, Senator, I do not. I think that there are certain times when the market is tough to recruit that we have to have those incentives to bring young men and women into the military. So, we need to have those tools to be able to man the force.

Senator JOHNSON. Now, in my business, we also employed recruiting bonuses, and they were most effectively paid out to employees, people that knew folks, understood the operation. In the past, recruiting bonuses actually had been legally paid out to members of the service, correct?

General GRISOLI. Correct, Senator.

Senator JOHNSON. But in this case, paying those bonuses to military personnel was illegal, improper?

General GRISOLI. There are many different ways something can be illegal. For example, the types of funds that are used. When we look at our inefficiency concerns, we look at the type of money, the purpose of the money that Congress gives us, and the time we are supposed to spend those dollars. And so that is what we took a look at, and if those are not done properly, it is illegal.

Senator JOHNSON. Now, as a manufacturer, I am always trying to drill down and find out what the root cause of this problem was. So, we have a recruiting bonus program, which on the surface makes sense and actually allowed you to recruit the number of individuals we needed. But then something went wrong. What was the breakdown? What was the root cause that something that may have been a good idea, a recruiting bonus, went across the line and resulted in fraud and criminal activity?

General GRISOLI. The breakdown, the fundamental breakdown, was in how they established and then executed the program. So, when you establish a large acquisition program of this nature, first of all, you have to have the right internal controls and processes in place. Some of the other parts that were challenging for the National Guard Bureau was their actual organizational structure that we found. So, the structure was improper. They are working to correct that and we have addressed that. The establishment and the plan, the acquisition strategy, was improper, so, therefore, that led to poor execution.

Senator JOHNSON. The last area I just want to explore is the authority of the Guard to actually utilize funds from this standpoint. Now, at least the previous recruitment bonus program was actually passed as a law by Congress, correct? And that was in what year?

General GRISOLI. That was in 2006, that Congress had the Bonus Referral Program.

Senator JOHNSON. And this program started the same year, correct?

General GRISOLI. It started prior to that.

Senator JOHNSON. It actually started prior to that.

General GRISOLI. Yes, sir.

Senator JOHNSON. So, I guess, let me ask Mr. Bentz here, have you looked at the legal counsel, the legal advice that the Guard relied on to institute this program for their authority?

Mr. BENTZ. Senator, we did not audit the authority under which the RAP program was established.

Senator JOHNSON. General Grisoli, have you looked at that?

General GRISOLI. Senator, the Guard relied on Section 10503 of Title X for our legal basis, which was their authority and responsibility to assist States. That particular area is ongoing review by us right now. We wanted to have our legal counsel take a hard look at that authority.

Senator JOHNSON. Now, at the time, did the legal counsel look at that statute and express a legal opinion that this was legal and authorized? Or was this something that the command at the time just took upon themselves and took a look at that statute and said, OK, we have the authority, and just moved forward?

General GRISOLI. At that particular time, we believe there was some legal counsel by the National Guard Bureau to their contracting office. The question in mind right now, was it the correct legal counsel to the Guard Bureau.

Senator JOHNSON. Well, is there documentation of that? I mean, are there legal written opinions provided to the procuring officer?

General GRISOLI. We do not have a legal opinion or opine of the situation at 2005, no, sir.

Senator JOHNSON. If that legal opinion was sought, it was just a verbal opinion?

General GRISOLI. I would have to presume, Senator, that that is what it was.

Senator JOHNSON. OK. I would really dig into that. I would want to find out exactly how this authority was assumed, on the basis of what legal opinion. If it was verbal, I would get testimony from the counsel that provided that legal advice. I think it is a legitimate question. I think it is kind of the heart of the issue here, too, just in terms of ongoing oversight, to prevent this thing in the future. So, certainly from my standpoint, I want that question answered.

General GRISOLI. Senator, we will do that, and as we review the basic authority for that, that will be part of our review.

Senator JOHNSON. OK. Again, I want to thank the witnesses for your service, for coming forward, and again, thank you, Madam Chairman, for this excellent hearing.

Senator MCCASKILL. Thank you.

Senator JOHNSON. Thank you.

Senator MCCASKILL. Let me followup on that a little bit. If there is a new program undertaken in the military, I was under the assumption that in the active branches, there was always the requirement of a written legal opinion for a program to begin, especially one that was embracing hundreds of millions of dollars of expenditures.

General GRISOLI. Madam Chairman, that is correct. When you establish an acquisition strategy, the Contracting Officer should always go and get a legal opinion on that strategy.

Senator MCCASKILL. But that did not occur here.

General GRISOLI. We do not have evidence of that occurring.

Senator MCCASKILL. And, is that because there is not a written requirement of that in the Guard as there is in the active branches, or is that because that requirement was disregarded?

Mr. BENTZ. Sir, I can talk to the extent to which the Guard Bureau, in their contracting process, sought legal review or did not seek legal review. We concluded that their efforts to seek legal review on the RAP contracts was insufficient. In certain instances, they did not seek legal review. In certain instances, they received a legal review that was neither dated, fully commented on, and/or questions or comments from the legal review fully resolved, ma'am.

Senator MCCASKILL. My friend from Missouri will be on the next panel and there is no question that I know that no one intended anything other than good to come out of this. We needed recruits. We were in a very stressful situation for command. We were, really, for one of the first times in our history, beginning to use the Guard and the Reserves in an operational capacity. They were being asked to do what they had never been asked to do before.

And so I am sympathetic to the command pressure but I need to be clear here that it was, in fact, command pressure that brought this about rather than a thorough vetting of this program and the way it was going to operate through normal channels of legal counsel and acquisition policy. Is that a fair characterization?

Mr. BENTZ. Senator, we did conclude that there was pressure brought from the ASM folks on the contracting folks to make RAP happen.

Senator MCCASKILL. OK. Let me go back. Let us talk about the contracting process, because this is particularly frustrating. I worked on contracting for years and I keep thinking, OK, we have really turned the corner, and then one of these issues turns up. Now, admittedly, this was back in 2005, before we really began focusing the entire military apparatus on basic core competency on contracting.

Now, I do not need to spend much time. I have been in briefings many times with your folks, General Quantock, about the fraud that occurred and the theft that occurred in the context of Iraq, and to a lesser extent in Afghanistan. We are doing better. We have actually got training for the contracting officer representatives (CORS). We stood up a contracting command. I think the leadership of the military now understands that you cannot have the attitude, ''I needed it yesterday, I do not care what it costs,'' because that is kind of what the attitude was.

But, talk to me a little bit about this contract and how bad it was. Was there anything they did that met the requirements of Federal procurement law as it related to the way this contract came about?

Mr. BENTZ. Our conclusion was, very little. There are actually three contracts associated with the RAP. Initially, the first Guard RAP contract was a task order placed off an existing marketing services contract, so outside the scope of that contract. As they moved forward, there was little acquisition planning, as referred to. In the award of the G–RAP base contract in 2007, there were processes that favored the incumbent contractor, did not actually account for full and open competition in that award.

Senator McCaskill. You are being very careful because you are an auditor, and I definitely understand, because having been an auditor, you never want to shade anything. But, let me state it plainly and see if you disagree with my statement.

Docupak task ordered off an existing marketing contract that really had nothing to do with this particular function. Then, when it came time for competition, Docupak had inside information that allowed them to compete in a way that was totally unfair to the other potential bidders on this particular contract, so, no surprise, they got the contract.

Mr. Bentz. I agree, ma'am.

Senator McCaskill. OK. Let us talk about leadership and fraud in this instance. There is evidence that one major general committed fraud, 18 full colonels, 11 lieutenant colonels, and dozens of other mid-level and junior officers. I need to know, and if you cannot give me specifically all of those today, I need to know for the record what has occurred in all of those instances in terms of holding them accountable. It is particularly egregious when it is our leadership, and that is why I hope they have received priority, and I would love you to speak to that, General Quantock.

General Quantock. Yes, ma'am. Actually, that was our first priority, is to look at all senior leader misconduct up front. So, in addition to age, we also looked at senior leader misconduct. I would have to take it for the record[1] to go back and break down all those cases. But, again, it was dollar value, it was age of the case, and, of course, our first priority was senior leader misconduct, before we looked at anything else.

Senator McCaskill. To your knowledge, have any of them gone to prison?

General Quantock. No, ma'am. To my knowledge, none have gone to prison.

Senator McCaskill. Have any of them lost benefits, to your knowledge?

General Quantock. No, ma'am, not to my knowledge.

Senator McCaskill. Have any of them been forced to resign from their service?

General Quantock. I would have to take that one for the record,[2] ma'am.

Senator McCaskill. OK. It is very important that we know that.

General Quantock. Yes, ma'am. Absolutely.

Senator McCaskill. I think we have learned one thing over the last 6 or 7 years of contracting oversight, and that is the way you really begin to change a culture that would allow this to happen is to have everyone see that senior leaders are held as accountable as a young member of the Guard who figured out he or she could scam the system and game this to make thousands of dollars he or she was not entitled to.

---

[1] The information from Mr. Quantock appears in the Appendix on page 66.
[2] The information from Mr. Quantock appears in the Appendix on page 66.

General QUANTOCK. I will tell you that one of the senior leaders, though, it was one case and it was for $7,500 because they brought in a doctor. In that particular case, the statute of limitations did rise up and the Assistant U.S. Attorney failed to go forward with the case because—it was not that the statute of limitations had then expired at that point, but by the time it went through the courts, it would have. So, I think that is also.

And also, the small dollar amount. Although to us it is abhorrent—to the Congress, it is abhorrent for senior misconduct, but for many Assistant U.S. Attorneys, it is more dollar value and bang for your buck than it is on actually who commits the offense.

Senator MCCASKILL. Well, the thing I am most concerned about is I understand that there are very few U.S. Attorneys, unless they work in the District of Columbia or someplace where they have primary criminal jurisdiction, that would bend over or pick up something off the floor for a $7,500 fraud because they typically are focused on much bigger cases.

On the other hand, the worst thing that could happen would be for senior leadership to go quietly into the night, and that is why I want to know, what tools do you have to make sure that everyone understands that there was punishment here? I mean, even if they are not going to prison, even if the criminal statute of limitations have run, I need to know what else you can do.

General QUANTOCK. Well, there are, of course, many administrative tools in the Secretary's kit bag, to include Promotion Review Boards at the very end of this chain to see if—did they serve at that particular last rank honorably, and it may impact, for example, what you talked about, future retirement benefits.

Senator MCCASKILL. What about the Uniform Code of Military Justice (UCMJ)? Is it applicable for any of these?

General QUANTOCK. Yes, ma'am. However, most of them were in the Guard and most of them are in Title XXXII, non-Title X status. So, it would fall to the Guard to prosecute many of these cases, or in many cases, it is going to even fall to the civilian jurisdiction, civilian courts, to take the vast majority of these cases.

Senator MCCASKILL. Well, for the leadership cases, I am thinking. I would like to explore that further, and we will do some questions for the record, because I have gotten very familiar with the UCMJ on another subject matter and I think it is really important that we utilize it aggressively when we have had leadership that may fall outside of the interests, because we have a lot of cases that have dual jurisdiction, as you well know——

General QUANTOCK. Yes, ma'am.

Senator MCCASKILL [continuing]. General. We have lots of cases where the civilian prosecutor could take it or the military could take it. And, frankly, when that occurs, many times, the civilian does not want it, as we have learned in sexual assault. Case after case, the civilian prosecutors say, "I will not touch that," and the commanders have said, we are going to go forward.

General QUANTOCK. Roger.

Senator MCCASKILL. We know that has occurred, literally——

General QUANTOCK. Yes, ma'am. Of course——

Senator MCCASKILL [continuing]. A hundred times in the last few years.

General QUANTOCK [continuing]. The subject at that time is in Title X——

Senator MCCASKILL. Right. So, you cannot——

General QUANTOCK. So that is the Title X-Title XXXII discussion that we always have when we want to take a case that we cannot. So, I agree with you a hundred percent, ma'am. We need to hold our senior leaders accountable, more accountable than anyone else, and we will take for the record[1] where we are at on that.

Senator MCCASKILL. And we may need to look at, in the Defense Authorization next year, at the UCMJ, because I know we are going to continue to focus on making sure we have it right there. It might be that we could do some things that would help.

General QUANTOCK. Yes, ma'am.

Senator MCCASKILL. Let us talk a little bit about oversight. This is an interesting part of this problem that I think is not immediately apparent to anyone who happens along this story. That is, the recruiters do not really work for the Army National Guard. They work for each individual Adjutant General in every State, is that correct?

General GRISOLI. Chairman, that is correct.

Senator MCCASKILL. So, what authority does the National Office of the National Guard have over these recruiters, if any?

General GRISOLI. Chairman, you are getting at some of the crux of the problem, which is the decentralized execution of this particular contract and not having special management oversight or internal controls, and that, I believe, and we have found, has caused many of the challenges.

Senator MCCASKILL. So, the bottom line is the recruiters in every State work for the Adjutant General (TAG) in every State who is appointed by that State's Governor and is responsible for hiring the recruiters and overseeing the recruiters.

General GRISOLI. The States have that requirement, and that is—the central National Guard Bureau or Army Guard assists them.

Senator MCCASKILL. So, that is why we see a wide disparity between some States and other States?

General GRISOLI. I think it is a training issue, because some States are better than others, and I think that causes a challenge in overall management.

Senator MCCASKILL. Could you speak to that, Mr. Bentz, about the differences in terms of the patterns that you might have seen or maybe it is General Quantock—because we have some States where it looked like a free for all, and then other States where it appeared that there was not this rampant fraud. Could you give us any insight as to what was the difference in management in the various States in terms of oversight of this contract?

Mr. BENTZ. I cannot. Our look at the oversight of the contract was really at the Guard Bureau and the folks at the headquarters level, oversight of the contractor. I cannot speak to——

Senator MCCASKILL. Can you, General Quantock, speak to the differences? We had a lot in Colorado. We had a bunch in Texas. There were other States that did not have as much. I mean, it is

---

[1] The information from Mr. Quantock appears in the Appendix on page 67.

almost like word got out and nobody was paying attention, and all of a sudden everybody thought, OK, the bank is open. Let us go for it.

General QUANTOCK. Ma'am, I have to take that for the record.[1] We looked at this in a holistic sense. We did not really dive down into actually the interaction between each of the States and really make a comparison.

Senator MCCASKILL. Well, I think we need to do that, because I think if we are going to hold people accountable, I think it is very important that in each individual State, the Adjutant General understands what happened under their watch and that they have primary responsibility for oversight and control over the recruiters, even though the program was designed in a way that it was very hard to have the adequate controls.

People knew this was going on. There is no way that there was not a culture of people saying, hey, here is the deal. There is a bounty and we know these people are signing up. My understanding is, we even had some high school counselors who knew that their kids were interested in the Guard, so they went on and signed up to take credit and get money for these enlistments, even though these kids were going anyway. Is that true?

General QUANTOCK. Yes, ma'am, that is true.

Senator MCCASKILL. OK. Let us talk about the lack of controls in the program itself. Mr. Bentz did your recommendations include ways to design a recruiting program with a reward for a recruiting bonus where you would have some control?

Mr. BENTZ. We did talk to changes to the contract, to the program, as far as the way the contract is set up and the fee that would be paid related to the contract. We did, obviously, look at the controls. The contractor, obviously, is responsible for controls over execution of the contract, and then the government has a responsibility to do quality assurance on the contract.

Senator MCCASKILL. How many investigators do you have working this right now, General Quantock?

General QUANTOCK. Ma'am, I have 60 full-time investigators working on this. We have brought in from the National Guard, from the Reserve, and some of our CID retiree rolls have come on. So, this is a task force, 60 full-time. Now, I also will tell you, many of our agents, or many of our other agents throughout the force are also working it. A total force of about 200, but 60 full-time.

Senator MCCASKILL. And would you state for the record the total amount of money you estimate the government has been defrauded under these programs?

General QUANTOCK. Right now, it is $29 million, but the question is—we have cleared about $203 million. There is a delta of $66 million that we still—and that is really the further investigations as we go on. But there is, at worst case, we believe, $66 million as we do the rest of the 21,000 that we have to basically vet through and run the criminal investigations, or run the investigations on. So, I would say there is about $66 million that are still out there in addition to the $29 million that we have already identified, ma'am.

---

[1] The information from Mr. Quantock appears in the Appendix on page 67.

Senator MCCASKILL. Twenty-nine plus 66, or 66 total?

General QUANTOCK. Twenty-nine plus 66.

Senator MCCASKILL. OK.

General QUANTOCK. That is worst case. Many of these folks will have done nothing wrong. These are the medium-and high-risk individuals that we talked about, and——

Senator MCCASKILL. So, it is every medium-risk——

General QUANTOCK. It is every medium-, every high-risk——

Senator MCCASKILL [continuing]. Came into the corral, you would end up——

General QUANTOCK [continuing]. For all fraud——

Senator MCCASKILL [continuing]. With close to a total of $100 million.

General QUANTOCK. Yes, ma'am.

Senator MCCASKILL. Which is unlikely, that all of the medium-risk cases are fraud.

General QUANTOCK. Yes, ma'am. I would call that very unlikely.

Senator MCCASKILL. Right. So, we are probably talking about, if we had to guess or die, around $50 million.

General QUANTOCK. Yes, ma'am. I think that is a good estimate.

Senator MCCASKILL. OK. What is the most that any single recruiter defrauded that you have been able to uncover at this point in time? What is the largest amount that somebody pocketed that was fraudulent?

General QUANTOCK. I want to say it is around $35,000, but I will tell you, we have one case with five individuals that is nearly a million, between five individuals.

Senator MCCASKILL. OK. What percentage of the medium-and high-risk cases that you have are at danger of running the statute of limitations?

General QUANTOCK. I have to take that one for the record,[1] ma'am.

Senator MCCASKILL. OK. And I think before we have—before I close this part of the panel, I think it is important that we look at what one of these fraud cases looks like. It does not matter to me which one of you takes this, but if you would give maybe two different examples of how this fraud occurred so we would have it in the record, so people could envision how this worked and how easy it was to pocket this money fraudulently.

General QUANTOCK. Well, ma'am, in your opening statement, you laid out well how this could have happened. Recruiters' assistants were basically anyone, and, of course, if they had access to a great deal of personal identifying information (PII) is what we refer to it—and if they were either by themselves, or they could be in cahoots with a recruiter—that is why we have to go through every single recruiter—but they could create an account, register an account, and then anybody that they thought may be able to—and they would be unknowing. They could come into the Army, or into the National Guard, and they never knew they gave up their PII. And that recruiter assistant would basically register them up.

And that is sort of how we go after the investigation piece. We have to go back and look at all the people they recruited and find

---

[1] The information from Mr. Quantock appears in the Appendix on page 68.

out, you were registered under this recruiter assistant. Did you give your personal information? Did you know that he was registering you to come into the National Guard? And, of course, the vast majority of these individuals, as we go through them, did not know that they had given their PII up to a recruiters' assistant.

Now, in the bigger cases, not only did they do that, they also were in cahoots with the recruiter, and that is the second type, where the recruiters' assistants were in cahoots with the recruiter. And you could tell that because many of the—when they went online to put their names in the system—they all had the same IP address. So, they either had the high IP address or they had many people using the same account information to put the money into.

So, that is why you can quickly vet through the low-and the medium-and the high-risk based on how the crime was expected to be——

Senator MCCASKILL. So, you go to the people who are in the Guard and you say, someone recruited you and got paid for it. Do you have any idea who that is? And they are saying, no, I do not know who that is, and nobody recruited me, and I did not give my information to this person.

General QUANTOCK. That is correct, ma'am.

Senator MCCASKILL. How would they have gotten this information other than from a recruiter? Maybe you could go hang out in the office and——

General QUANTOCK. Well, another example——

Senator MCCASKILL [continuing]. See who was walking in and then try to claim that you recruited them.

General QUANTOCK. Well, if you have a recruiter that is in this, you go into the office, you want to recruit, you give your personal information to the recruiter. The recruiter has his recruiters' assistants out there, and what they can do is give that personal information to the recruiter assistant. He registers and they cut the $2,000 in half.

Senator MCCASKILL. I get the kickback part. I get that a recruiter could easily set up 15 recruiters' assistants who were all his good friends or family members and he could sign up everybody he recruited to get his family members paid so he could get a kickback. But what about the cases where the recruiters were not enabling this? How would a recruiting assistant get the personal information and get this money unless they were a high school counselor or something like that?

General QUANTOCK. Exactly the point. High school counselor or high school principal with all the PII available, knowing their seniors are getting ready to join, want or are interested in joining the military, they already have ready access to the Personal Identifying Information, and that is usually how we saw it, and there are many ways, and a lot of times, they would get the PII, and the person unknowingly would give the PII to them, but did not know what they were going to do with it.

Senator MCCASKILL. I see. We have a number of things for the record, and one of them is I do want to look at the highest rates of fraud on a State-by-State basis so that we can provide some guidance and oversight to these Adjutant Generals, because I am sure the Adjutant Generals are just as mortified and embarrassed as anybody is that knows that we have the best Army in the world and the finest National Guard that anyone would hope for. I want to make sure that we are not forgetting that there is a whole piece of this that is not in Washington.

Is there anything else that I have not covered with you or a question I have not answered that any of you want to address before we dismiss you and hear from the next panel? Yes, General Grisoli.

General GRISOLI. Chairman, I just want to ensure you that we look forward to working with the Subcommittee and yourself as we continue to work through this very complicated challenge. We are concerned, also, about the fraud and the mismanagement and we will work with you openly to make sure that we get this right.

Senator MCCASKILL. Well, once we finally began to open the spigot, you all have been very cooperative. I think there was at the beginning a little bit of denial as to the necessity for our Subcommittee to get all of this out in the open, and it is painful, but sometimes you have to rip the band-aid off and that is the only way you really get it fixed.

Mr. Bentz, you had one more thing, and then I will turn it over to Senator Ayotte to ask as many questions as she would like.

Mr. BENTZ. No, ma'am. I was just going to say there was nothing further.

Senator MCCASKILL. OK. Great. Thank you all for your work, and Senator Ayotte, do you have some questions?

Senator AYOTTE. I want to thank the Chairman very much. This is an incredibly important issue, and I know that you have asked many of these questions.

I am trying to understand, and I think the Chairman already covered it—but why it took from CID so long, from 2007 to 2011, to request the Army Audit Agency to begin a fraud risk assessment. So, that is a long time when you have fraud going on.

General QUANTOCK. Yes, Senator, and I will walk you through that. Again, in CID, we conducted over 43,000 felony investigations. If you look at how this started, in 2007, we had two CID cases that were related to this, five in 2008, two in 2009, and then 10 in 2010. So, you can see, these are dots and they were across the United States. So, they would not have been picked up systematically until 2010, when one of our agents in the Huntsville office realized there is some vulnerability in this and we are seeing a little bit more of this kind of problem. So, we need to really take a systematic look at this whole contract, and that is why it was referred to AAA in 2011.

Senator AYOTTE. So, what about the command structure? Where was the oversight of this? So, I know it is done by a contractor, obviously, but when the funds started going out the door much faster than you would have anticipated, as I understood they did——

General QUANTOCK. I would have not had oversight of that particular——

Senator AYOTTE. Yes, but I am talking——

General QUANTOCK. We look at it from a criminal——

Senator AYOTTE [continuing]. About in the command structure. One of the things I think we struggle with quite frequently is things that are delegated to contractors, and sometimes the contractors—and I am not being critical of the contractor here. My point is that there are other places where we can be quite critical of contractors across the board, Snowden, other things that this Chairman, I know, has spent a lot of time on.

How are we conducting oversight of these contractors, so not just your, the transfer to looking at the investigation of it, but there is an oversight function. When the money starts going out the door a lot faster, how is it within the command structure that we did not pick up on that as a raw indicator right there, that something was not quite right, as oversight within the system?

Mr. BENTZ. Senator, you are correct. On behalf of the Guard Bureau, the oversight of the contract insufficient. The Contracting Officer's representatives that were responsible for that oversight, they believed that the contractor was responsible for the oversight and control of the program.

Senator AYOTTE. They thought the contractor. They did not realize that they—that we had to oversee the programs——

Mr. BENTZ. Correct.

Senator AYOTTE [continuing]. Because the contractor does not take the same oath that all of you take in terms of overseeing what the contractor does.

Mr. BENTZ. Correct. Obviously, the contractor has a responsibility to ensure that it has a system of quality control to——

Senator AYOTTE. Right. But they report to someone within the agency, with the Guard Bureau.

Mr. BENTZ. Exactly.

Senator AYOTTE. OK. One thing that, Lieutenant General Grisoli, in your written statement, you wrote that, quote, "funds were lost due to systematic weaknesses, a general breakdown in sound business processes, and wrongdoing." So, one is oversight within the system and other weaknesses. Can you tell me a little bit about that, and the one thing that I think about as we look at this problem is if the problems are systematic, how can we have confidence that the Army does not have similar problems in other programs when we are talking about systematic problems? So, if you can help me with that, I would appreciate it.

General GRISOLI. Senator, first, on the question reference other issues, you talked a little about the oversight and the structure. The structure, we found to be not sound.

Then, when we took a look at how, and we spoke a little bit about this, how there was oversight for each one of the States, because it was kind of decentralized, what sort of internal controls were placed on that, those were not where they should have been.

And then the way we prevent something like this happening in the future is we have what we call Program Management Reviews. We had our Procurement Executive do a Program Management Review on the overall contracting system of the National Guard Bureau. We are working very closely with them to implement that now. They have provided us a corrective action plan. We have accepted that plan and now they are implementing that plan. But we have directed that and they are moving out. So the systematic, the systemic ones that we are concerned about, we are working on fixing those right now so we do not have another sort of——

Senator AYOTTE. So, you are looking across systems——

General GRISOLI. Exactly.

Senator AYOTTE [continuing]. Not just this particular issue.

General GRISOLI. Yes, Senator.

Senator AYOTTE. And, General Quantock, you talked about how the rising rate of incidents really flagged, came to eventually flag this in terms of the criminal investigation. Why is it, though, and maybe you answered this but it would help me to understand, when the money started going out the door on a faster rate and that was not flagged, for example, in the Guard Bureau piece, why was it not that somebody before it got to you all asked the question, well, why is this money going out the door so much faster than we thought it would last us? I am just trying to understand that, because that would have been a question that I would have had, had I been, or any of us, in that situation, wondering, our money is supposed to last us this long and it seems to be going a lot faster than, really, it was supposed to.

General GRISOLI. Senator, I believe you are getting at another issue as far as internal controls and the feedback loop and properly providing that oversight to track that, and that was another weak area.

Senator AYOTTE. So, someone just was not tracking that, or how was it not flagged?

Mr. BENTZ. Senator, part of the responsibility on the Contracting Officer's representative, they did look to the burn rates of how they were going through the funds. They just did not call flags based on what they saw on the burn rates.

Senator AYOTTE. That did not flag for them?

Mr. BENTZ. That did not flag.

Senator AYOTTE. But, this was burning the money much faster than we thought, was it not, as I understood it?

Mr. BENTZ. I do not believe that was an issue across the program, that the funds were being used more quickly than anticipated.

Senator AYOTTE. Maybe I misunderstood that, but——

General QUANTOCK. I think there is also probably no common flags on the cause, because when you look at the recruiters, Senator, and the recruiters' assistants, about 105,000 estimate, 81,000 are probably OK.

Senator AYOTTE. Sure.

General QUANTOCK. We have gone through and vetted them. So, when you start looking at the totality of it, there was not really— no red balloons that were up there for us to identify until later on down the road. Even the burn rate, because if the burn rate was below the authorization, then it probably did not send any signals up, either.

Senator AYOTTE. Thank you. I appreciate it. Obviously, this is something that we need to make sure that the systematic controls are put in place, but also that within the command leadership that this becomes a priority of oversight when we do have contractors.

And I think one of the bigger challenges we face, too, is there is sort of this feeling, when the contractor is doing it, they have it covered, and it has created—there have been multiple examples where—not just within the Department of Defense (DOD), in other agencies, we have seen some pretty significant problems with this.

So, we have to create—if there is going to be a contractor—I think we should ask ourselves, do we need a contractor for this, No. 1. But, No. 2, if there is going to be a contractor, so that the leadership is clear what their oversight responsibilities are with that contractor.

So, I want to thank the Chairman for holding this hearing and really bringing this topic to light, and thank you all for what you do for us.

Senator MCCASKILL. Thank you.

I want to make sure I clarify this for the record. Mr. Bentz, there was a determination that the whole program violated the Anti-Deficiency Act, correct?

Mr. BENTZ. They are currently doing a review at our ASA, or Assistant Secretary of the Army for Financial Management and Comptroller, over potential Anti-Deficiency Act violations——

Senator MCCASKILL. OK.

Mr. BENTZ. Yes, ma'am.

Senator MCCASKILL. So, that has not been determined yet?

Mr. BENTZ. That is in process. I believe the completion timeframe for that is October of this current year.

Senator MCCASKILL. OK. Do you want to add anything to that, General?

General GRISOLI. Chairman, it is a preliminary right now. It is with the Office of Secretary of Defense (OSD) and the formal should come out on October 14.

Senator MCCASKILL. October 14?

General GRISOLI. Yes, ma'am.

Senator MCCASKILL. OK. We will mark our calendar. Thank you all very much. I appreciate your service, and to have somebody in law enforcement and an auditor on the same panel makes my day anytime, so thank you very much.

Senator AYOTTE. Madam Chairman, may I submit something just for the record——

Senator MCCASKILL. Sure.

Senator AYOTTE [continuing]. So that it is clear, because there really was a problem with, as I recalled reading, with the rate in which this contract was spent that was not flagged sooner, and I have a document that I would like to submit for the record.

So, if you all could just address that question for me again in light of this document, I would appreciate it.

General GRISOLI. Yes, Senator.

Senator AYOTTE. In written answer.

General GRISOLI. Yes, Senator.

Senator AYOTTE. Thank you. I appreciate it.

Senator MCCASKILL. Thank you all very much.

We call our next panel of witnesses. [Pause.]

I will tell you what. Why do not you all stay standing and we will do the oath first and then I will introduce you and it will keep you from having to get back up.

Do you swear that the testimony you are about to give before the Subcommittee will be the truth, the whole truth, and nothing but the truth, so help you, God?

General VAUGHN. I do.

Colonel JONES. I do.

Mr. CRANE. I do.

Colonel HENSEN. I do.

Senator MCCASKILL. Thank you all.

If you would be seated, let me introduce this distinguished panel, first, beginning with Lieutenant General Clyde Vaughn. He retired as the Director of Army National Guard in June 2009 after 40 years of outstanding service to the Guard and to the U.S. Army. As Director, General Vaughn oversaw a force of 350,000 soldiers in 50 States, U.S. Territories, and the District of Columbia, and developed and implemented all programs and policies affecting the Army Guard. General Vaughn previously served as Deputy Director of the Army Guard and Assistant to the Chairman of the Joint Chiefs of Staff for National Guard matters.

Colonel Michael Jones retired from the U.S. Army in 2012, after 27 years of service, and now works in the civilian market to provide veterans, military spouses, and wounded warriors with employment opportunities. Prior to retiring, Colonel Jones served as Division Chief of the Army National Guard Strength Maintenance Division and held positions in the Office of the Secretary of Defense and the National Guard Recruiting and Retention Office.

Philip Crane is the President and co-founder of Docupak, a marketing company founded in 1998 with expertise in program management, information technology, and the development of promotional materials. Prior to forming Docupak, Mr. Crane held several positions related to marketing, advertising, sales, and logistics.

And Lieutenant Colonel Kay Hensen manages all Federal contract compliance programs for Docupak. She is retired from the military and previously served in the United States Army Reserve, the Ohio Army National Guard, the National Guard Bureau, and the Montana Army National Guard. During her military service, Lieutenant Colonel Hensen served as a Contracting Officer and expert in contractual planning, proposal writing, compliance, and budget forecasting.

I would like to thank all of you for appearing today. We appreciate you being here. I know that you are anxious to help us get to the bottom of this and make sure that we keep this from ever occurring again. I will take my home State privilege, General Vaughn, and turn it over to the Missourian in the group.

TESTIMONY OF LIEUTENANT GENERAL CLYDE A. VAUGHN (RET.),[1] FORMER DIRECTOR, ARMY NATIONAL GUARD

General VAUGHN. Chairman McCaskill, it is a pleasure to be here. I really mean that. I look forward to testifying and I am proud that you have called this hearing.

As you know, I have talked with your staff quite a bit last Tuesday. I had not seen any of the reports that were out there. They got them for me. I had already turned in my statement, so I am going to cover some of the things that were in the memorandum from your staff, which are very helpful.

OK. So, the idea for this comes from the States. We were Arkansawing [phonetic] about January 2006 and the Adjutant Generals brought it to me and said, "If we could recruit from within,

---

[1] The prepared statement of Mr. Vaughn appears in the Appendix on page 48.

if you manage to get to be the Director, then we could make a big difference.'' Now, what were they talking about? In fact, that particular individual was Major General Hank Cross out of Mississippi. When I became the Director, we were 20,000 soldiers under strength, and as you have said several times, they had a lot of stuff going. To give you an idea, we had over 100,000 mobilized all over the world at one time. We had Katrina and Rita hit and we put 50,000 more on the Southern coast. And when we looked around, we only had 275,000 available out of the whole thing. So, we had to get our strength up.

We had thought about this comment from the TAGs and we had set out to see if we could figure out how to do that, because it——.

Senator McCaskill. TAG, just for the record, General, is the acronym for the Adjutant Generals in each State.

General Vaughn. Exactly.

Senator McCaskill. Right.

General Vaughn. So, we put the plan together. Again, I have not done any interviews on this, but there was a PAT that was called in from the States. It was led by my deputy, General Grass. It was staffed very well. If you are asking about the legal and contracting piece, they never worked for me.

But there were chops on a document someplace because nothing could possibly come up that far from what you call ASM through the G–1 through the Chief of Staff. You are exactly right. There is always a summary sheet that shows the chops on it. And the two chops, of course, that you have to have are contracting and legal, and the authorities, you account for your people to do the right work and have all that in place. And when it finally gets to you, you have a back brief.

We cut an order off of that back brief, got it out to the States. They were very excited about it. There were some other events. I have seen some verbiage and some reports that want to know why I accelerated. That would be a good question to ask, maybe, later on. I want to get through my statement now.

But, we moved out and kind of the rest is history. It was a great recruiting program and I do not think you will find too many people that will not state that. We have a recruiting commander in the back from one of the States that is an expert on this program and I think he will tell you exactly that. Some States did a wonderful job with this.

I did not know of the irregularities, and, of course, you cannot blame me, because the CID, the Commander just told you how this occurred. We thought we had a great program running. And, I tell you, I reviewed documents on a daily basis, what was happening in the program, and I had a lot of things on my plate, no excuse. Once a month, we had video teleconferences (VTCs) with all TAGs, with all Adjutant Generals and all the recruiting staffs, and I told them, I said, we have to catch the first peckerwoods who get out here and mess this thing up for everybody and we have to prosecute them quickly. And I did that 18 months in a row. And if I did not do it, Frank Grass did it as my deputy, or a guy named Jim Nutall. You can find it, exactly where that was done.

Now, you asked a question a while ago about the relationships of the TAGs. Obviously, they have command and control. Well, how did that work? What could we have done? We had done the same thing that Secretary McHugh did with the entire program when he was alerted to a real problem out there. If we would have known that there was a real problem in this program during the time I was there, we would have shut a State down, which would have been a major embarrassment, because, you see, the power we had where we were at was the power of the purse strings.

The burn rate was what it was. I mean, I think the report says we got a soldier for every piece of money that went out there. And, oh, by the way, the $300,000 that is referred to in your report, that recruited 130,000 soldiers, if you look at that, that only comes up to about $2,400 a soldier.

So, what I am telling you is, at the end of the day, if you are buying tanks and you wanted to buy a thousand tanks, if it had been tanks, we would have gotten a thousand tanks for the money we put out there. I mean, sometimes that case or that point is lost.

Now, there was fraud between people that really knew there was fraud, and I do not think when they find them they have any trouble prosecuting them, because, like you say, the trail is there. But we did not have a chance to make a mid-course correction because we did not know.

Now, who else did not know? Well, if you think about this, the Secretary of the whole Army rolled the same program out along with the United States Army Recruiting Command (USAREC) over the top of the Army Reserve. Now, last time I was around, the Army Reserve's big program was under the control of the Army under USAREC. You need to check that out, because I am not sure. I have been retired for quite a while, but that is the way it was.

So, you ask yourself, how is it that the Director, and, oh, by the way, the two deputies, and, oh, by the way, the Chief of the Bureau and the Secretary of the Army Chief's staff of the Army do not know about this in order to make a mid-course correction?

The other thing, of course, you are going down the road on is what were the authorities that they were operating under with all their lawyers—and again, that is a legal and contracting issue that belonged over with the National Guard Bureau.

Now, to look at your report real quick, and I know I am running short, but this is very important, especially for some of the things that you covered a while ago. They covered the fact that the CID learned about this in phases all the way out and so it was hard to pick up. Here is an amazing thing, and sometimes we lose sight of this, and I think I have heard you talk about it a couple times and also had the CID agent.

They open the cases up on everybody that received payments, of 106,364 individuals, right out of your report. And they also told you a few minutes ago that they had cleared the cases with the exception of 20,000. There are still 20,000 out. That leaves the figure of 1,219 that they are now investigating or have been adjudicated, which means, looking at it from another way around, which I do not see anyplace, and based on what he said, it means approximately 84,800, which is 98.5 percent, of our great soldiers and some of the greatest patriots in America did the right things, and there were some dunderheads, about 1.5 percent, that have caused us the problems. And by causing us the problems, they shifted money around. And at the center of this, for the most part, were full-time recruiters.

But, we do not lose sight of the fact that it was a tremendous recruiting program and we got the people. And we reached 350,000 soldiers in May 2007. I retired in 2009, and I was dismayed to see that article in the Washington Post, and I kept thinking, what is there that we missed? How in the world did that happen?

And so I am pleased that you have had the hearing. I would look forward to talking to anybody in great detail about what occurred here so it can be sorted out.

The one thing, I am not sure it would even have made a difference, but one thing I guess I should have, looking backward at it, is had an informal relationship with CID. Now, CID, of course, has a command line to the Chief of Staff of the Army and Secretary of the Army. For some reason, I guess if I had to do it—and I know they do not talk to anybody, because you have been in this business where they are trying to prosecute folks, but somehow, I probably, if I had done anything over again, I would have probably done that, and I still do not know if we would have been able to make course corrections mid-term because of the way it occurred, and it looks like it really peeled out a little later in the cycle past my retirement.

Senator MCCASKILL. Thank you.

General VAUGHN. That concludes——

Senator MCCASKILL. Thank you, General. We will have some questions for you. Colonel Jones.

TESTIMONY OF COLONEL MICHAEL L. JONES (RET.),[1] FORMER DIVISION CHIEF, ARMY NATIONAL GUARD STRENGTH MAINTENANCE DIVISION

Colonel JONES. Chairman McCaskill, Ranking Member Johnson, and Members of the Subcommittee, thank you for inviting me to testify before you today to help educate and provide more context of the program.

First of all, my name is Michael Jones. I am a retired Colonel from the Army National Guard. I had the honor to work and lead the Army Strength Division between the years of 2006 and 2009.

The G–RAP program, to me, I believe, was an excellent program, and as I sit here today, as the General had talked about, dollar for dollar, it was one of the best bang for the buck, as you referred to earlier, ma'am, that the taxpayers had.

In 2006, the Department of Defense released a report that said that the Army was paying, on average, $18,327 for every new accession, and G–RAP reduced that down to approximately $2,400, a savings of $15,927, roughly. Now, if you were to say 130,000 accessions, as documented in your staffers' memo yesterday, you can quickly do the math on what that savings was. Well, it is well over a billion dollars of potential savings and real savings for the government.

Despite these savings, and I just have recently heard, when Jackson e-mailed me the notification last Friday, that the Committee had heard or been told of alleged widespread fraud, which,

---

[1] The prepared statement of Mr. Jones appears in the Appendix on page 52.

according to the numbers—and, ma'am, Jackson did provide us, and I do not know why the Army did not have it, we do have the State-by-State breakdowns of those percentage of recruiters and those that are still to be adjudicated. So, it is completely analyzed and I am sure that the Army can be provided or will be—or I will provide them what I have on that State by State.

In my opinion, this was a very successful program, perhaps one of the most effective peer-to-peer recruiting programs. After all, these were not our full-time Guard members. These were those citizen soldiers that worked and lived and went to church and school exactly in the places where we needed to be. And in 2005 and 2006 and then on into the Afghanistan surge, recruiting was so difficult and the ability to just pile on deeper and deeper with advertising money and more direct mail, it just was not working. And so the Adjutant Generals came up with a program some have said was ill-conceived. Ma'am, I think it was brilliantly conceived because it allowed us to use the greatest resource we have to tell the Guard's story, and that is that traditional Guard soldier.

All I have seen is a claim that there are roughly 100 adjudicated cases out of the 130,000. I did hear and respect the general officers that testified, ma'am. I know there is more to be done and it is a process that goes on there. But, based upon what the staffers provided and running the numbers by State, it shows that—and I think General Vaughn talked about it—approximately 1 percent of potential fraud there, and, ma'am, that is 1 percent too many. One case is one case too many.

It was only yesterday that I realized, or received information which informed that there was alleged direction of the methods and pressure put on contracting. It has also been alleged that there was undue influence and command pressure. Ma'am, this is sheer nonsense, and here is why.

According to the reports I have read, those claiming that this happened—these people claiming that had at least seven options available to them if they felt some vague pressure. No. 1, they could have looked at me, Colonel Jones, and said, ''You are not our boss.''

No. 2, these warranted Contracting Officers could have done the acquisition plan correctly.

No. 3, these same warranted Contracting Officers could have gone to their senior level of command, of which I was not in. I was on the Army Guard side of command working for my three-star, not on their side of command working for their three-star.

Or, they could have gone to the NGB–IG. Or, ma'am, they could have gone to the Army Inspector General. Or, these warranted Contracting Officers could have simply not done it because, ma'am, I had no authority, no control, no supervision, no oversight, and no power to direct them or make them do anything inappropriate.

In closing, ma'am, the few comments that have alleged that the concept was not well conceived, I would like to be able to—hopefully, that will come up and talk to you about that.

In my opinion, Senator, we have done a great job of cooperating with your staff, Jackson and his team—I hope he will corroborate that—and look forward to attempting to address the value of G–

RAP, address what I think are some maybe misconceptions, address any issues of weakness.

Thank you, ma'am.

Senator McCASKILL. Thank you so much. Mr. Crane.

TESTIMONY OF PHILIP CRANE,[1] PRESIDENT, DOCUPAK

Mr. CRANE. Good morning, Chairman McCaskill, Ranking Member Johnson, and Committee Members. Thank you for allowing me the opportunity to testify today. I am Philip Crane, President of Docupak, an integrated marketing company founded in 1998 that provides marketing and production capabilities within a single firm to meet client needs with program management design, packaging, production, inventory control, warehousing, and distribution. Our company also provides other services, including information technology, print on demand, and development of promotional products. Docupak does not sell prepackaged products, but tailors our solutions to each individual client's needs.

Madam Chairman, at the outset, I would like to correct the record to reflect that it has come to my attention in preparation for my appearance today that we previously stated that the staff that we contacted Army CID initially. As a matter of fact, our review has indicated that an agent within the Defense Criminal Investigative Service (DCIS) contacted us and focused on the program with various investigative agencies. We have at all times remained available and transparent to government authority.

Today, I am here to discuss the program that we provided to the National Guard Bureau for the Guard Recruiting Assistance Program. Since the inception of G–RAP, Docupak has established and informed government and contracting offices of internal controls used to mitigate fraud, waste, and abuse, and through these efforts, we identified and suspected—we identified and reported suspected fraud cases to the Army CID for investigation and potential prosecution.

While the contract was terminated for convenience in 2012, we have continued to assist Army CID and other government agencies in identifying potential fraudulent activities. To date, we are aware of approximately 28 convicted RAs out of the more than 300,000 that participated in the program. Since its inception, G–RAP has achieved in excess of 149,000 total accessions and achieved a 92 percent successful ship rate to basic combat training.

We have consistently made our program records available for review and audits. As I have mentioned in my letter to the Committee requesting the opportunity to testify, our records and our employees remain available to the Committee Members at the staff's convenience.

Throughout the history of the contract, Ernst and Young was retained to audit and to provide assurance that our company's financial statements were precise, complete and accurate. Those audits include an examination of evidence supporting the amounts and disclosures in our financial statements and an assessment of the accounting principles used by our company.

---

[1] The prepared statement of Mr. Crane appears in the Appendix on page 58.

I am truly grateful to the Committee to allow me to testify today. Thank you.

Senator MCCASKILL. Thank you, Mr. Crane. Colonel Hensen.

TESTIMONY OF LIEUTENANT COLONEL KAY HENSEN (RET.)[1], CORPORATE COMPLIANCE OFFICER, DOCUPAK, AND FORMER CONTRACTING OFFICER, NATIONAL GUARD BUREAU

Colonel HENSEN. Good morning, Chairman McCaskill. I am Kay Hensen, former National Guard Bureau Contracting Officer and now the Corporate Compliance Officer of Docupak. I would like to take a brief moment to provide some background on my experience directly related to my current position at Docupak, where I am responsible for contract procedures and ensuring compliance with applicable laws and regulations.

Before my employment with Docupak, I served for 27 years in the military. During my tenure in the military, I served various duties, including logistics, administration, contracting, contract policy, and supervisory positions. My last duty assignment was as the supervisory Contracting Officer for the Montana National Guard. After receiving my post-employment clearance from the Montana National Guard Ethics Counselor, I accepted a position at Docupak conducting contract audits, reviewing and updating compliance requirements, and developing corporate policy guides for government purchasing.

I have more than a decade of experience in government procurement from both a government and corporate perspective. My areas of expertise include Federal Acquisition Regulation (FAR), long-term contractual planning, proposal writing, compliance, negotiations, and budget forecasting. In addition, I have a Level III certification in contracting from the Defense Acquisition University. I received my Bachelor's of Science (BS) degree in sociology from Regions College and a Master in Business Administration (MBA) from Touro University.

Today, I am here to discuss my duties as both a Contracting Officer for the National Guard Bureau as well as my current role at Docupak. Thank you for allowing me to participate in this hearing.

Senator MCCASKILL. Thank you.

I will go over your numbers and see the 1-percent, but our numbers say the G–RAP program, in total, was $338 million. The Reserve RAP was $28 million and the Active Army was $7 million. You add that up, it is just shy of $400 million. And you just heard the General in charge of all criminal investigations in the Army say that his estimate was this is going to be $50 million. Well, I am not a mathematician, but $50 million of less than $400 million is a hell of a lot more than 1 percent. I mean, north of 10 percent of the total amount of money spent on this program has been identified as fraud. Now, I do not think you think that is acceptable, that level of fraud.

Colonel JONES. No, ma'am.

Senator MCCASKILL. Correct?

---

[1] The prepared statement of Ms. Hensen appears in the Appendix on page 61.

General VAUGHN. Ma'am, I was talking about if you take the total number, the 106,000, and you subtract out what they have investigated, you get to a figure of 86,000. Of that, they have cleared 84,800. What he said in here was about 81,000 or 82,000 soldiers they have cleared. And what that means, that 1,219 that is on your document is about 1.5 percent of that first tranche of 86,000 people.

Senator MCCASKILL. So, what you are saying is——

General VAUGHN. I am talking——

Senator MCCASKILL [continuing]. The number of people who participated in this——

General VAUGHN. Yes, ma'am.

Senator MCCASKILL [continuing]. Was small, but the amount they ripped us off for was pretty darn big.

General VAUGHN. It could be. It certainly could be, and they could have shifted it around. I do not see the numbers because I do not have access to that.

Senator MCCASKILL. OK. I wanted to make sure I understood that.

General VAUGHN. No, I certainly was not claiming it was 1 percent that was fraudulent.

Senator MCCASKILL. Yes. OK.

General VAUGHN. OK.

Senator MCCASKILL. And, listen, I get it that if you incentivize people with money, you are going to get results. I get that. There is no question that you got results with this program. I do not think anybody is here to argue that. What we are here to argue about is whether or not it was designed in a way that would have prevented people making money while not adding value.

General VAUGHN. Right.

Senator MCCASKILL. It is one thing if somebody goes to their church and recognizes that there is someone there who is an engineer that we need in the Guard and they say to them, hey, have you thought about the Guard, and they bring them in. It is a whole another ballgame when the recruiter is providing personal information so they can grab some money when that person signs up and does not even know the recruiter.

I know you all are here, and I am proud of you for being here and you have cooperated, but we have to realize that this could have been prevented. We could have stopped this from the beginning. This did not have to happen. All you had to do is when a recruit came in, they would be required to name their recruiter.

General VAUGHN. If you are asking the question, and the responsibility for that happens to lay down at the Adjutant General's Office through their command chain. You hit a great point a while ago. Many, States are going to come out of this, in my view, pretty good, and why? Because they had great leadership and they had a lot of integrity and they continually talked about the things that you have just addressed. And it all hurts us to hear that, but that is exactly what the issue is.

Senator MCCASKILL. OK. I have to argue with you a little bit, Colonel Jones. You said that it is $18,000 per recruit. Well, you do not do away with some of that base cost if you go totally to a bounty system. In that $18,000 is the administrative costs of actually processing people through the system, correct?

Colonel JONES. Chairman McCaskill, I did not mean to argue with you and certainly would never try to argue with you. I was just referring to the number that was put out as the cost per recruit at the time in 2006 that was rising steadily. All of the factors, whether that included the manpower cost——

Senator MCCASKILL. Advertising——

Colonel JONES. Yes, ma'am.

Senator MCCASKILL [continuing]. Marketing——

Colonel JONES. Yes, ma'am. But, I do—to the best of my ability, it does not include the manpower cost. But, yes, ma'am, with great respect, ma'am, $2,400, there was still some additional cost to process them. Yes, ma'am.

Senator MCCASKILL. Right. Then the question is not was the $2,400 nice and low, but is the $18,000 too high, and what I would love to do at the end of this whole process is to come up with some recommendations that would be adopted by the National Guard Bureau and by the States and by the Army and the Army Reserves as to how you could run a recruiting program with adequate controls.

Colonel JONES. Ma'am, may I address that?

Senator MCCASKILL. Yes.

Colonel JONES. To echo what you had said, ma'am, the 1-percent—I just wanted to clarify, because I did not want to in any way mislead you or be disrespectful—was I meant the number of people that were involved.

Senator MCCASKILL. The bad apples.

Colonel JONES. Yes, ma'am. I am a soldier. I sacrificed. My family sacrificed. And my buddy on the left and right of me, they were not all bad. That was what I was trying to say.

Senator MCCASKILL. Of course.

Colonel JONES. And, yes, ma'am, a dollar misspent is a dollar misspent, and I apologize for that.

Back to your question about effectiveness and cost effectiveness, we were converting three-to-one, so for every three what were called potential soldiers, when a recruiting assistant brought in someone, that was one. The next two that came in, so we had three. For every three that were brought in, one became an accession. On all of our other advertising programs, ma'am, and I have enormous documentations down to this particular direct mailing had all of this metrics that I will provide to Jackson, we had that on everything we did. The traditional advertising, which Congress was so gracious—during these years, ma'am, not you, but the Congress was giving us——

Senator MCCASKILL. A huge amount of money.

Colonel JONES. It was, what can we avoid to do to avoid a draft, because of all that was happening, and all of the other traditional methods that had worked, ma'am, honestly, for 20 years——

Senator MCCASKILL. Were not working.

Colonel JONES. They were not, and they converted at 18-to-1. And that was in General Schoomaker's 2007 posture statement. And so, ma'am, this is called a high-risk program. And, in my heart, during this period, my boss in the Army and the Congress, we believed—I do not want to put words in the Congress' mouth, but I believed that the highest-risk program was deploying our combat units at 70 or 80 percent end strength, and that is where we were. And that does not excuse anyone, as you said, scheming the system.

And, ma'am, during this period, the General talked about that during the time that I was there, that he found out two, five, and two. So, CID only knew about two, five, and two, and they were not even briefing us on what was going on. If we had known that there was even two, five, and two during the time that I was there, that would have been enough to, I think you said, send up a red balloon or flag to say, let us take a look at this and find out——

Senator McCASKILL. Right.

Colonel JONES [continuing]. Where can we make this better, so that what you said is so that the goodness of the program is not shelved because the bad actors that are out there.

Senator McCASKILL. Right.

Colonel JONES. And, ma'am, honestly, we had recruiting assistants that were in college. They were in the middle of the market. Our recruiters were not there, but they were there.

Senator McCASKILL. No, I understand. Our problem here is not whether or not the idea was a bad idea.

Colonel JONES. Yes, ma'am.

Senator McCASKILL. It is whether or not the execution of the program——

Colonel JONES. Yes, ma'am.

Senator McCASKILL [continuing]. Was done in a way to prevent fraud. That is why we are here.

Colonel JONES. Yes, ma'am, and——

Senator McCASKILL. And so let me move on——

Colonel JONES. Yes, ma'am.

Senator McCASKILL [continuing]. And let me ask Colonel Hensen, with your background, have you read the audit that Mr. Bentz did?

Colonel HENSEN. I did read it one time, ma'am.

Senator McCASKILL. OK. So, I am curious, since you are an expert in FAR, did you read that this program did not comply with almost any of them?

Colonel HENSEN. I left National Guard Bureau in 2006, in January 2006, so all I can speak to is what was going on in the office during my tenure, and I believe when I made my decision to execute that first task order, that I was in compliance with the FAR. And I did have legal and I had policy and my division chief approval in writing prior to making that award.

Senator McCASKILL. So, you had legal in writing that you could do on a task order for Docupak to do this?

Colonel HENSEN. That is correct.

Senator McCASKILL. Well, you need to help us find that.

Colonel HENSEN. I have no access to it at this point. I did call the Contracting Office to make——

Senator McCASKILL. Because that lawyer is in trouble, because there is no way you could task this off a marketing contract.

Colonel HENSEN. Under the terms that we were executing that marketing contract to maintain maximum flexibility in developing new programs, new initiatives in order to find a way to recruit in a completely different environment, that contract was used, basically, to investigate and conduct contract research on different new initiatives, and this started off as a lead generation initiative.

Senator MCCASKILL. Were you there when this contract was competed after the task order?

Colonel HENSEN. No, ma'am, I was not. I was in Montana at that time.

Senator MCCASKILL. Mr. Crane, I want to thank you for your co-operation and thank you for correcting and giving us the information that it was, in fact, the criminal investigation side of the Army that began this as opposed to your company.

Having said that, you were here and you heard the testimony from the first panel that you all got an insider position on this competition. I want to give you the opportunity to address that. Would you quarrel with that, that you had information that no other bidder had?

Mr. CRANE. Well, the bit of information that we did have that no one else did was we were the incumbent and we had past performance. But beyond that, that was all the advantage we would have had.

Senator MCCASKILL. So, you are maintaining that the only thing about the competition that was unfair was that you were the incumbent?

Mr. CRANE. Yes, ma'am.

Senator MCCASKILL. But, we have incumbents all the time and the auditors do not find that there was an unfair advantage, that there was information an incumbent had that was not shared with the other bidders.

Mr. CRANE. I am not aware of any information that we would have had that would have been not made public during the solicitation.

Senator MCCASKILL. Well, evidently, the auditors found some that was, so we will hunt that down for you and make sure that you have a chance to review.

I have other questions I need to get to, but some questions just arose from your testimony. I am a little worried, frankly, and I get the points you are making and you have made them very well, that there are a lot of things about this program that made sense. I get that. But, what worries me a little bit is that I am reminded of what I heard around contracting in Iraq from the generals. Not my problem. Not in my command. Not my issue. The notion that this was a problem for the warranted Contracting Officers, do you see any problem with that? Do you agree that we need to figure out how to make sure every commander in every situation realizes the contracts that are being executed that impact their command have to be their problem?

General VAUGHN. No, I agree with you. As I discussed earlier, probably, there has to be a staffing document to come all the way up. All our staffing documents carried a chop, from each one of the organizations, whether it was outside of our organization or not. And in this particular one, it was outside of our organization. But it would have carried a chop from them. And to hear Ms. Hensen talk about this thing that there has to be a document out there, I would say it is absolutely right.

And not only that, it had to be coordinated with the same Army that went down the same road in RAP. I mean, that is why if you follow the bouncing ball, I do not quite understand this. It was Army that stood side by side with us and rolled out Army First when we used the G–RAP program, me and the Secretary standing side by side. Now, how can everybody with a national press conference, stand there and look at that and then some years later say, well, we got that all wrong authority-wise and on and on and on. There is more questions that need to be asked——

Senator MCCASKILL. There is no question, and I agree——

General VAUGHN. Yes, ma'am.

Senator MCCASKILL [continuing]. Because the Army did roll it out, although much later than you did, and obviously it was shut down much more quickly. You all had been in operation for a number of years and their time—I think I just said that the amount they spent was $7 million compared to $338 million in the Guard——

General VAUGHN. Yes, ma'am.

Senator MCCASKILL. But, that does not change the fact that they signed up, and so there should have been those legal authorizations there just as we are asking those questions of you.

General VAUGHN. That is exactly right, and I think from a regular authority standpoint, the only they could use was their Deployed Entry Program (DEP), I believe, and that was only, like, 500 soldiers. Those were young soldiers waiting to go to basic training, and so they were not Title X soldiers yet and they used them in the same program. But they only used it for 500. But, the fact of it is, the Army Reserve moved into the same program, having to use the same authorities with the same oversight.

And so as I look at this years later, and anybody that has ever worked with me all the way through, we had never done anything where we pressured someone to do something wrong. And it is an integrity issue and we would not put up with it.

Senator MCCASKILL. In a November 2005 Operations Order that you issued that established G–RAP, it identified fraud as a potential problem in the contract. Who was in charge? Who did you look to as being primarily responsible for finding or detecting the fraud that you identified when you rolled the program out?

General VAUGHN. When we rolled the program out, as you have said, we did a risk assessment. We did a hot wash, a red teaming on that, brought all the States in. And, of course, that is exactly where those pieces in the op order came from, and they are all even today talking about how that rolled out. We gave that to the individual States and TAGs and then we set—I have spent 1 day a month all day with all 54 States and Territories four regions explaining the whole thing. And in every instance that we went through one of these regions, I would say, OK, now, do not forget, do not kill the goose that laid the golden egg here. Stay on top of it. I emphasized every piece of this. And every recruiter out there understood that, and there were States that took the direction on this and moved out and did great things. And then there were other States, as I discussed with you, that the really heartbreaking thing is we did not have a place to make a mid-course correction in this and shut down a program or go in and do some real deep soul searching about what they were doing. And you can only imagine the embarrassment in a State if they were singled out and we had shut them down. We would not have had a problem with that.

So, who do we hold responsible? We hold, as the CID agent, or Commander, pointed out, the ultimate responsibility is that TAG, and he has command responsibility down through his recruiting commanders.

Senator MCCASKILL. So, Colonel Jones, did you disagree with the audit finding that there was no effective internals in the program?

Colonel JONES. I did, ma'am.

Senator MCCASKILL. You did disagree with that?

Colonel JONES. Yes, ma'am.

Senator MCCASKILL. And what were the effective controls that were there?

Colonel JONES. Ma'am, the Operations Order clearly spelled out, the FAQ sheets, the G–RAP document spelled out in great detail. It went through and issued, or talked about every question, scenario, level of responsibility, tasked to be taken all the way down to the non-commissioned officer in charge (NCO–IC). That is the E–8 who runs the recruiters. I mean, it had specifically in there that they were to conduct continuous fraud risk assessment, take proper corrective actions, and notify chain of command, and all the way up the chain of command to the Recruiting and Retention——

Senator MCCASKILL. Well, it is one thing to say you should not have fraud in the program, but an effective control would be something that would ferret out when somebody was sharing personal information in order to get a bounty on somebody who they had not recruited. Was there any control like that at all in this program?

General VAUGHN. Ma'am, the structural piece that is built in is the United States Property and Fiscal Officer (USP&FO) in every State. That is a Title X officer put out there that is owned by the Chief of the National Guard Bureau and detailed out there for that. And inside of his or her——

Senator MCCASKILL. That is a Fraud Prevention Officer for those of us——

General VAUGHN. Absolutely. He owns all of the pieces. Now, how is it possible that, for instance, the center core of all these things revolved around full-time recruiters? How is it possible as a front-line supervisor that if there is an investigation going on, or a commander, that he would not have known about the investigation and come up on the other side to the Chiefs of the National Guard Bureau, which you know my ex-boss, General Blum, you know what that would have done over there on that other side. That is an explosion. He did not know—I do not see how he knew it. I never talked to him.

But what I am telling you is, that chain did not work. For what reason, I do not know. Today, I still do not know whether CID ever coordinated and talked to every officer—and I am not trying to push any bucks anyplace. I am just telling you, there were redundant looks and redundant places that we should have been able to get the word and make a correction to this exercise. It did not happen.

Now, they say they did not see it, either, and I am telling you, when I left in 2009, it looked like a clean program. They did not pick it up until 2011, obviously.

Colonel JONES. Chairman, there was one thing that we talked about that we believed would have prevented this, one system, one internal control check. Now, before I get to that one, we had internal control checks within the division. We used the Army's system of record called the Amateur Radio on the International Space Station (ARISS). So, that was check No. 1. Was the accession loaded in there? Did it correlate to recruiting assistance, recruiter's Social Security number, their accession load number?

Then we said, OK, that is not good enough for payment. Let us wait until it is actually loaded into the Standard Installation and Division Personnel Reporting System (SIDPERS) database, which is the Army Guard's system of record for personnel, because we wanted to say, what happens if there is a system error and something dropped? A payment would be made. That would have been a payment in fraud. So, we waited, and that was approximately 30 days.

Senator MCCASKILL. Right.

Colonel JONES. And then we said, OK. Let us give it another 30 days, because, what we used to call it in the recruiting world, buyer's remorse. A kid gets in there, he is ready to go. Bad news on the——

Senator MCCASKILL. Colonel Jones, I get you explaining all that. I get you had controls in there to make sure nobody got paid until somebody actually joined. That is the control you are talking about. We are not talking about that kind of control that was needed.

We are talking about the kind of control to prevent a situation in which somebody was going to join anyway and somebody made five-grand off him joining. That is the fraud. It is not that somebody did not go all the way through accession and report to basic and actually become a member. It is, in fact, that for people who were going to do that anyway, somebody was paid who did not deserve it. That was the fraud.

So, I get that you had that control in——

Colonel JONES. OK, ma'am.

Senator MCCASKILL [continuing]. But nobody put a control in, and did you realize at Docupak that there was no control for that?

Mr. CRANE. Well, may I take just a moment and walk you through the controls that we did have in place?

Senator MCCASKILL. Sure.

Mr. CRANE. The first primary function was to determine whether an RA was eligible to participate in the program. That fact was determined by government supplied data which would give us the duty status of an individual, and if they could not participate, if there were certain programmatic things that they were doing within the Guard, such as if they were associated with a recruiting office, that would eliminate them.

Senator MCCASKILL. Right. You had to eliminate the recruiters.

Mr. CRANE. Yes, ma'am. So, the first action was to try to make sure that there is a separation off of ARISS files.

And then, second, we would bounce last names versus last names of recruiters to see if it was a spouse of a recruiter or a sibling or a dependent of a recruiter. This was community-based, so we did run across that. So, they would be disqualified.

Second, when an RA nominated——

Senator McCaskill [continuing]. Which were essentially your subcontractors.

Mr. Crane. Yes, ma'am. That is correct. So, in order to nominate a potential soldier, you would have to be in an eligible status——

Senator McCaskill. Right.

Mr. Crane [continuing]. And you would have to put in PII of that individual.

Senator McCaskill. Right.

Mr. Crane. In addition to that information, we required—in the beginning, it was a radio button, seven questions, where you met them, how you met them, and a series of questions. After the program was instituted, I do not remember the exact date, but we did alter that to be able to put in free typing which would require the RA to fill out all of that information prior to it being recognized in our system that it was a legitimate nomination.

Senator McCaskill. OK. So, let me make sure I understand this. In the beginning, you had to answer questions, where you met this person—what else besides where you met them?

Mr. Crane. What is most likely their Military Occupation Specialty (MOS) they would be interested in——

Senator McCaskill. OK.

Mr. Crane. And I do not remember all seven, and I apologize. What would be a likelihood of a timeframe of him or her——

Senator McCaskill. OK. And then you converted that to them having to write some kind of summary as opposed to answering questions.

Mr. Crane. Yes, ma'am.

Senator McCaskill. OK. And what did the summary have to contain?

Mr. Crane. It would be those same questions, but they would not be fixed questions. They would have to free-type that information in.

Senator McCaskill. What kind of check was there that what they put in was true?

Mr. Crane. Well, that leads me to where I was headed, and you made mention of it just a few moments about, about trying to recognize and identify things that could have helped eliminate some of the potential fraud. In looking backward and thinking about this an awful lot over the last week and a half, if we had created an automated response—it could have been an e-mail, because we had to get the potential soldiers' contact information—if we would have sent out a verification e-mail to that potential soldier who had been nominated basically restating the facts that had been put into the system by whom it had been put in by, where they would have to certify the information that we had was legitimate, I think it would have gone a long ways, because——

Senator McCaskill. This is what kills me about this. This is basic. You just assumed that whoever was typing this in was telling the truth, and nobody ever checked to see if they were lying. You are handing out millions of dollars, no questions asked.

Mr. CRANE. I would just like to clarify one thing. We did have coordinators on our staff and those individuals were making anywhere from 25,000 to 30,000 phone calls a month, either reaching out to the recruiting assistants to verify information that they had put into our system, and also making attempts to contact the potential soldier.

Senator McCASKILL. Well, it has to be really hard to find the soldier at that point in time.

Mr. CRANE. That is correct.

Senator McCASKILL. Calling them is going to be hard.

Mr. CRANE. Yes, ma'am.

Senator McCASKILL. And, if you are going to call a liar and ask him, are you telling the truth, guess what they are going to say? "Yes." They are not going to say, "No, I lied." Did it say on the form, after they typed this in, that you could go to prison if you lied there?

Mr. CRANE. Yes, ma'am. That was in part of our——

Senator McCASKILL. And that did not stop.

Mr. CRANE. No, ma'am.

Senator McCASKILL. Obviously, I think you would need to figure out a kind of control that would not require you to get hold of them in person in light of what we were asking them to then do. I mean, they were in basic. They have been over the country. But this is why I am frustrated——

Mr. CRANE. Yes, ma'am.

Senator McCASKILL [continuing]. That these kind of controls, either through contracting at the beginning or through oversight through the program, were never put in place. And there was a lot of stovepiping here.

General, you were looking at numbers, and you were looking at your contract requirements, and there was an assumption that Fraud Prevention Officers in the States were aware of what they specifically needed to be looking after. Frankly, they could have taken a random sample of the recruits, and pretty quickly, they would have found out that there was fraud going on. So, that is what is so frustrating about this.

I think it is really important for me to point out this quote that you have in your written testimony, Colonel Jones. You said, "Potential wrongdoing on the part of contracted individuals were not believed to be within our authority."

Colonel JONES. Yes, ma'am. I should have said subcontractors, because we were not allowed to talk to subcontractors. It should have been subcontractors, and that was at the State level to do the Fraud Mitigation Plan, the followup, the investigative work to check on what was happening via the contractors.

The only way that we could have known for sure, ma'am, was if we had had access to a recruiter's bank account, even non-sequentially named, and could have had a list of bank accounts, and then we could have monitored any transactions, any deposits from a contractor. That would have been the ultimate catch-all to say, OK, that is wrong because you know you are not allowed to be in the program. When discussed, we were told, you cannot have access to anything like that without a court order with a known suspicion of wrongdoing.

Senator MCCASKILL. Well, at that point, did you feel comfortable contacting the Criminal Investigation Division of the Army for assistance?

Colonel JONES. Well, ma'am, we were told—or, we were not told. I never knew—again, when I was there, the numbers that were available were two, five, and two, that there were a total of nine incidents going on.

Senator MCCASKILL. So, you did not have any sense that this was going on whatsoever.

Colonel JONES. Well, I had the—what I just told you. It is the same knowledge that CID had, that in 2006, there were two; in 2007, there were five; and in 2009, there were two more. It was not until 2010 and 2011 where they started to see it, and then it started to become more prevalent——

Senator MCCASKILL. Prevalent.

Colonel JONES. Prevalent, yes, ma'am. Thank you. Sorry.

Senator MCCASKILL. Well, we have dozens and dozens of pages of deficiencies that the auditors found in the contract, and we have a contractor that does not appear to have taken seriously the potential fraud problem here. And I understand, it did not impact your bottom line, other than the fact that it went away. I assume this was a profitable contract for your company.

Mr. CRANE. Yes, ma'am.

Senator MCCASKILL. So, is there anything that I have not asked about that you feel has been characterized unfairly here? I really do think that there is a systematic failure along the way here of people to talk to one another. I think the chain of command got in the way on this one. I think that the decentralized nature of the Guard contributed to the problem. There is a wide variety of things that actually occurred here that allowed this fraud to flourish, and we have to figure out how to fix it without blowing anything up that we do not want to blow up, and that is where I need you all to give us input. I need you to talk about how you have some kind of ability, some kind of authority over contracting, how you take more responsibility for fraud other than just saying it is the TAGs, because it is not the TAGs' money. This money is all coming out of the central budget, right? This money came straight from Washington, did it not?

So, should we not have some kind of fraud oversight in the Guard Bureau that has the specific responsibility of doing spot audits for programs with this kind of money that is being paid out to civilians who sign up online?

Colonel JONES. Yes, ma'am.

Senator MCCASKILL. There is not that position now, I assume.

Colonel JONES. I do not think so, not that I am aware of.

General VAUGHN. No, not that I am aware of. I do not know how the Joint Staff is organized, because, as they deal down to touch the United States Property and Fiscal Officers, for the most part, they mirror whatever is out there. So, I do not know if it exists over there. It certainly did not exist with us other than providing overall guidance, and I think we nailed it pretty good in our op plan, in our op order. In fact, I read somewhere in one of the reports, and I did not know what the heck a QASP was, I mean, we had lots of things. We were dealing with the $40 billion worth of equipment upgrade and deploying lots of soldiers——

Senator MCCASKILL. No, there is no question, your plate was full. That is why I am saying, it appeared that your fraud control was having a VTC with Adjutant Generals every month saying, if you get caught with fraud, you are going to screw this up. Well, with all due respect, General, that is not really aggressive fraud control. I think you were a powerful guy and you were in charge of the Guard Bureau, and you did have the power of the purse. But, having a VTC once a month and saying, do not have any fraud, did not appear to get it done in this instance. And I think we probably need to have a more aggressive fraud structure at the Guard Bureau.

General VAUGHN. Well, I think that is an excellent point. There is no doubt about it. We certainly would not argue with it at all.

Senator MCCASKILL. Great.

General VAUGHN. But, it still gets back to the issue of some States did a remarkably good job, and that is going to come out. And one of the things I look forward to when you finally bring this to an end is what happened out there in all the States.

Senator MCCASKILL. Well, we are going to continue to work on that, and we will publish a ranking of the States when the criminal investigations are completed by virtue of statute of limitations or the investigations being complete. Now, they have a lot of work still to do. In fact, CID let us know that some of these investigations might go all the way to 2016. So, it is going to be a while before the dust settles and we really figure out how many people we are going to put in jail on this. But, at that point in time we are going to publish a report card and we will go after the States that did such a poor job at this.

General VAUGHN. If you can really make a difference—and I really hate to see, in spite of everything that has been written about the program, I hate to see the baby thrown out with the bathwater. You asked something of Mike a while ago. I viewed the whole program as a test program as to whether we could move in and cut down the total number of recruiters in our force.

Now, when you do this math if we took, say, the 4,000 recruiters and cut them to 200 and made them general managers out there in the States—and I was working this issue, but we had to make sure that we could pull the whole load and recruit it with the G–RAP force and we basically proved that. But, if you did that, and if you were after 50,000 recruits and you paid them, just using $3,000 for the math, that is $150 million.

If you took the same 4,000 recruiters and say—and do not use the 18,000, take the other piece out of it, because now I am giving you the admin load in there, and you save the retired pay accrual and panel outs and the whole thing, and just say it is 100,000, and you know as well as I do it is much more than that, OK, that is $400 million up against 150 using this other system.

And then to get out the bigger issue, what if you took all of the Army's stuff, for instance, and just used one advertising system rather than three, and, oh, by the way, what if you could move that over to where that was the program to recruit folks, and that is what we were doing with Active First with Secretary Geren and we proved that we could do it——

Senator MCCASKILL. Well, listen, I think all those——

General VAUGHN. So, the cost savings is in the billions.

Senator MCCASKILL. Yes, and those are all good ideas, and I will convey to Guard leadership currently and to the Joint Chiefs and to the Secretary of Defense that there are better efficiencies we can realize out of our recruiting system. I think we have wasted a hell of a lot of money on a lot of things that have not worked. And I am not saying that the premise of this program is not valuable. But I will guarantee you this. I am going to yell at the top of my lungs if somebody tries to roll out this program without fraud control in it again, because that is what happened. This program got rolled out and implemented without fraud control, and you cannot do this kind of program without fraud control.

I know that we can sit here all day and talk about the value of the premise, but execution is the problem here, the way it was drawn up without controls embedded in it, whether it is more fraud prevention at the States, whether it is oversight of fraud prevention at the Bureau, or whether it is requirements in the contract in terms of recruits having to sign off as to who recruited them. There are a variety of things that could be done. I think we need to get to the bottom of all this and get it straightened out before we even start talking about rolling out this program again.

But, we are not going to end this hearing without recognizing there is value to the premise. It is a lot more efficient to send people into neighborhoods and to send people into churches and to send people into college campuses, and members of those communities can sell the Guard much more effectively than putting the name on a video game ad. I am all for that. I am not big on the video game ads, just so you know.

Is there anything else anybody wants to add for the record before we conclude the hearing? I really appreciate all of you being here. We will have followup questions for the record, and this will be a continuing area of focus of investigation for the Subcommittee until we finally get to the bottom of all the fraud that has occurred. I particularly want to reiterate on the record, until we find out how many of these leaders, how many of these colonels, the major general that has been implicated, how we make sure that they are held accountable, as they have done a great disservice to the men and women they lead.

Thank you very much.

Colonel JONES. Thank you, ma'am.

[Whereupon, at 12:06 p.m., the Subcommittee was adjourned.]

APPENDIX

RECORD VERSION

WRITTEN STATEMENT BY

LIEUTENANT GENERAL WILLIAM T. GRISOLI

DIRECTOR OF THE ARMY STAFF

BEFORE THE

SENATE COMMITTEE ON HOMELAND SECURITY

AND GOVERNMENTAL AFFAIRS

SUBCOMMITTEE ON FINANCIAL AND CONTRACTING OVERSIGHT

ON "FRAUD AND ABUSE IN ARMY RECRUITING CONTRACTS"

FEBRUARY 4, 2014

Chairman McCaskill, Ranking Member Johnson, and other distinguished members of the subcommittee, thank you for the opportunity to discuss the Army's Recruiting Assistance Program and the comprehensive Army efforts to detect, analyze, and investigate allegations of fraud. Accompanying me is Major General David E. Quantock, the Army Provost Marshal General and Commander of the United States Army Criminal Investigation Command as well as Mr. Joseph P. Bentz, the Principal Deputy to the Army Auditor General.

Before I discuss the particulars of the Recruiting Assistance Program, I wanted to let you all know that the accusations of fraud and other potentially criminal actions surrounding this program are as disturbing to us as I know they are to you. That is especially so given how within the past few years the Army has had to make some very difficult decisions in prioritizing the funds available to us. We have worked incredibly hard to squeeze every ounce of value from the funds Congress – all of you – provide. In this case, funds were lost due to systematic weaknesses, a general breakdown in sound business processes, and wrongdoing – none of which we will tolerate. So you have my commitment that we will do whatever it takes to put this right, and as you will hear today, we've already done a lot. We will also punish those who have broken the law, and recoup what we can.

The Recruiting Assistance Program, or RAP, was created in 2005 as an innovative way to bolster Army National Guard recruiting efforts in an unfavorable recruiting environment. At the time, tens of thousands of servicemen and women were required to serve extended tours of duty because of a shortfall in troops to relieve them.

The program offered "referral payments" to "recruiting assistants" that referred enlistees to the Guard, Reserve, or Active Component. The idea was to use "peer-to-peer" recruiting to increase the Army's recruiting footprint. This effort was coordinated by a contractor, Document and Packaging Broker Incorporated, or Docupak.

All components of the Army implemented a form of RAP for various periods of time: the Army National Guard from 2005 to 2012; the Army Reserve from 2007 to 2012; and the Active Army from 2008 to 2009. The total program cost was approximately $459.4M: $408.7M in the Army National Guard; $42.6M in the Army Reserve; and $7.9M in the Active Army. All told, the Army enlisted over 150,000 new recruits through this program. Although the Guard and Reserve met or exceeded recruiting goals soon after implementation, the program was continued without modification. The Active Army discontinued the program once recruiting goals were met in 2009.

In 2007, Docupak alerted the United States Army Criminal Investigation Command (CID) to possible fraud in the Recruiting Assistance Program. CID initiated several potential fraud case reviews. As the number of fraud cases associated with RAP grew over time, in 2011 CID requested the United States Army Audit Agency begin a Fraud Risk Assessment of the program. Upon learning the Army Audit Agency' preliminary results in February 2012, the Secretary of the Army immediately cancelled the Recruiting Assistance Program, directed the recovery of the remaining unexecuted RAP funds, and issued a comprehensive directive to aggressively examine and investigate this complex issue. This directive, issued on February 9, 2012, directed the necessary review and investigative action to determine ultimate responsibility and accountability for the failures in the RAP, and to initiate appropriate corrective action and preventative measures. Among other things, the directive tasked:

- The United States Army Audit Agency (AAA) to provide a Fraud Risk Assessment and systematic review of the various (all Army components) RAP to include the contract vehicles;

- The Assistant Secretary of the Army for Acquisition, Logistics, and Technology (ASA (ALT)) to review contracting procedures;

- The Assistant Secretary of the Army for Financial Management and Comptroller (ASA (FMC)) to determine possible violations of the Anti-Deficiency Act; and

- The Army CID to investigate individual criminal accountability.

The Secretary was updated by my predecessor on July 1, 2013, and on September 24, 2013 I updated the Secretary of the Army on actions taken as a result of his February 9th directive. He subsequently signed another directive building upon his February 9, 2012 directive to establish corrective actions and ensure individual responsibility and accountability. Many of these actions are ongoing today. Here is a status summary:

- The Assistant Secretary of the Army for Manpower and Reserve Affairs (ASA (M&RA)). Completed providing copies of RAP era policy, guidance, memorandums, and regulations related to recruiting policy, as well as names of the individuals who had responsibility related to recruiting during that period to The Inspector General (TIG).

- ASA (ALT). Completed providing copies of policy, guidance, and regulations related to service contract policy, administration, and oversight of service contracts in the RAP era to TIG. ASA (ALT) also reviewed the draft National Guard Bureau (NGB) and Mission and Installation Contracting Command Corrective Action Plans in response to the ASA (ALT) Program Management Review. Finally, ASA (ALT) concluded there had been a general breakdown in sound business practices from requirements definition through contract invoicing, and determined statutory, regulatory and policy requirements had been disregarded. ASA (ALT) issued a directive to all Army contracting activities requiring the inclusion of a Federal Acquisition Regulation Clause, Contractor Code of Business Ethics and Conduct, in full text in all contracts. ASA (ALT) is also working with the NGB to develop proper organizational structure, to include oversight, and execution plans for NGB procurement and contracting functions.

- ASA (FMC). Submitted the formal anti-deficiency act (ADA) report to the Army Office of General Counsel for review. The formal report lists the number of Army National Guard ADA violations at 280 with a potential associated dollar value of $829M. The formal report encompassed all recruiting initiatives reviewed, not just the RAP. This report should be completed in October 2014.

- TIG. Continues to work assignment of accountability by interviewing personnel from ASA (ALT), ASA (M&RA), the United States Army Reserve Command (USARC), and NGB. TIG reviewed over 1000 documents and completed 27 interviews, with potentially 50+ interviews pending. TIG is actively attempting to determine whether there were any senior leader oversight failures, and if so, who was responsible for those failures. TIG investigations are expected to conclude in April 2014.

- NGB. Submitted their comprehensive Corrective Action Plan to ASA (ALT) addressing all their Program Management Review findings for approval. They are also exploring with ASA (ALT) the feasibility of recouping funds related to fraudulent activity. NGB cancelled the National Guard Federal Acquisition Regulation Supplement and issued the new National Guard Acquisition Manual in 2012. They replaced the Head of Contracting Activity and the Principal Assistant Responsible for Contracting.

- CID. Continues to investigate and coordinate prosecution of criminal activity; to date CID has initiated 559 criminal investigations involving 1219 individuals and has evidence to believe the individuals fraudulently received a total of over $29M which is owed to the US Treasury. As of January 27, 2014, 104 individuals have been held accountable through either the courts or through administrative action by the Army. CID is also exploring the possibility of civil and administrative contractual remedies that may allow for recouping more of the fraudulent RAP payments. They will complete their preliminary assessment of the 12,106 recruiters and 94,329 recruiting assistants to determine criminality in the fall of 2016.

- AAA. Determined the NGB failed to satisfactorily perform acquisition planning, solicit and award contracts, administer contract actions, and oversee contractor performance. AAA provided the names of individuals found to have violated program rules (with no evidence of criminality) to the components for administrative action.

Again, the Army takes this issue very seriously and we are committed to working with Congress on this matter. Already we have responded to requests for information and documents by your Subcommittee. In addition we have executed several briefings to oversight Committee Professional Staff Members. You have my assurance we will continue to keep you all informed.

In summary, the scope of the Recruiting Assistance Program investigations, reviews, and audits encompasses the entire United States Army. This issue is both complex and far-reaching. The Army has taken aggressive and comprehensive steps leading to corrective actions to prevent future occurrences. The Army is committed to fully determining how this situation developed and identifying individuals who should be held accountable. We are making good progress and I am confident the end result will be substantially improved recruiting and contracting processes in the National Guard Bureau and across the entire Army.

Ms Chairman, Mr. Johnson, and other members of the committee thank you for your time and interest in this matter. We are committed to working with Congress as we move forward on this matter. We look forward to your questions.

STATEMENT OF

LIEUTENANT GENERAL CLYDE A. VAUGHN, USA (Ret.)

BEFORE THE SENATE COMMITTEE ON HOMELAND SECURITY AND GOVERNMENTAL AFFAIRS

SUBCOMMITTEE ON FINANCIAL AND CONTRACTING OVERSIGHT

FEBRUARY 4, 2014

Chairwoman McCaskill, Ranking Member Johnson, and other distinguished members of the Subcommittee, thank you for providing me with an opportunity to appear before the Subcommittee today at the hearing entitled, "Fraud and Abuse in Army Recruiting Contracts." In the letter of invitation I received from the Subcommittee, dated January 24, 2014, it advised that the:

> "...purpose of the hearing is to examine reports of pervasive fraud, abuse, and mismanagement in the award and administration of contracts for the Army National Guard's Recruiting Assistance Program (G-RAP). In particular, the hearing will examine reports indicating a widespread breakdown in oversight and accountability, and the failure to follow multiple laws, regulations, and policies. The hearing will also examine reports that millions of dollars were distributed fraudulently to Army National Guard members."

Specifically, the letter requested that I address the above topics, as well as my involvement in the launching and management of G-RAP as the Director of the Army National Guard.

I served as the Director of the Army National Guard from June 2005 until my retirement on June 30, 2009. As requested by the Subcommittee, a brief biography is attached to this Statement. In addition to the information contained in this Statement and my biography, I am prepared to answer questions posed by you and the other distinguished Members of this Subcommittee based on my personal knowledge and experience with the G-RAP program from its inception up to the date of my retirement in 2009. After my retirement date, I had no involvement with the program and have no personal knowledge of any developments or events occurring after 2009, which are the subject of this hearing. Furthermore, during my tenure as Director, I never received any information or reports about any money being fraudulently distributed to any Army National Guard members with one single exception, based on my best recollection. In connection with that one exception, I was advised that the individual involved was being prosecuted. On the other hand, I was very much involved with the launch of the G-RAP program in November 2005, and its operation through June of 2009.

The genesis of the program can be traced back to an ARNG Commanders' Conference that took place in Arkansas in January of 2005, at the behest of several Adjutants General. As conceived, it was designed to be a recruitment tool and a supplement to the recruiting activities of the full-time recruiters. The G-RAP program was not designed as a lead or referral program and it was never conveyed as such; rather, it was a recruiting program with a sponsorship component. The program was based on the "Strength From Within" concept utilizing the unique individual strengths and values of the ARNG soldiers to instill, educate, and recruit their peers.

The thought behind it was that citizen soldiers in the Guard were uniquely situated in their communities to identify potential quality recruits among their fellow students and fellow workers, an advantage that full-time recruiters did not have available to them. Moreover, from a budgetary standpoint, the cost of the incentive payments to these soldier-recruiters was so much less than the overhead costs of supporting the full-time recruiters so that, in time, it might be possible to reassign and return some of the full-time recruiters to other duties such as logistics and even combat readiness. To understand fully the need for this unique program, I believe it is important to step back a moment and consider the national environment in which it was conceived. In 2005, our Nation continued to face conditions unique in American history in the protracted global war on terrorism. The need for large numbers of fully-trained combat troops with supporting personnel was at an all-time high. The challenge of recruiting soldiers, in the best of circumstances, bears an inverse relationship to general economic conditions. When the economy is robust and jobs in the civilian sector are plentiful, recruiting can be difficult. When the economy is stagnant, and unemployment is up or rising, recruiting is less challenging.

In 2005, prior to the recession, the economy was healthy and recruiting was down. The numbers speak for themselves. When I became Director that year, manpower strength had been on a steady decline and the low point was reached on July 1, 2005, with ARNG manpower at 330,312, well short of the congressionally directed end-strength of 350,000. At the same time, over 100,000 ARNG soldiers were mobilized for federal Active Duty. Then, in late August 2005, Katrina, a Category 5 hurricane, struck and devastated the southern portions of Louisiana and Mississippi and the Gulf Coast generally. This required an additional 50,000 troops to meet these emergency circumstances. It was imperative, that if we were to continue to meet all mission requirements for the Nation, we had to succeed in achieving our appropriated strength number of 350,000 troops.

In putting the program together, considerable time was spent on evaluating the potential areas of risk, including fraud, and recommended courses of action. When the program was launched with the OPORD in November of 2005, it even identified as a potential risk the scenario where a full-time recruiter might take an enlistment and give credit to a G-RAP recruiter who had no active involvement with the potential soldier, telling him to claim credit and then split the $1,000. Thereafter, as the program was rolled out for implementation by the various States under the ultimate leadership and authority of each Governor, we consistently and repeatedly emphasized the need for monitoring and controls against the possibilities of fraud. I personally reviewed data on the program every morning and met with my program managers weekly. In addition, I conducted monthly VTC's with Adjutants General and recruiting officials of all 54 States, territories and the District of Columbia. Also, all of the appropriate approvals were obtained from those offices charged with vetting legal and contract authority issues. These were offices outside of my command.

From a recruiting standpoint, the G-RAP program was widely viewed as an enormous success because, with it, we were able to achieve the appropriated strength number of 350,000 troops by April 2007. In fact, all components of the Army implemented the program successfully for various periods of time. The Army Reserve utilized the program from 2007 to 2012 and the Active Army from 2008 to 2009. To my knowledge, none of the senior leaders were apprised of any wholesale fraud.

Going forward, it is my hope that the basic concept can be salvaged with appropriate safeguards in place to prevent fraud. It has shown itself to be an effective tool for recruiting with a potential for cost savings.

Testimony of Mike Jones, Before the Senate Financial and Contracting Oversight Subcommittee on Fraud and Abuse in Army Recruiting Contracts

February 4, 2014

Chairwoman McCaskill, Ranking Member Johnson, and members of the Subcommittee:

Thank you for inviting me to testify before you today.

I am Colonel retired US Army Mike Jones. I was invited to discuss the Recruiting Assistance Program. I am unable to fully address the reports of alleged widespread breakdown in oversight and accountability and alleged failure to follow multiple laws, regulations and policies, as I had never seen any of these reports until your staff gave them to me late Friday night. I was unable to process all the hundreds of pages of information in such a short time. Additionally, there were many documents referenced in the documents that were not provided. I can discuss my involvement in the launching and management of the G-RAP.

According to my officer record file and trying to remember all the dates from that long ago I do remember being the Deputy Division Chief in 2005 and becoming the Division Chief in late 2006 and served until some time in 2008 and detailed to other areas at that time. Due to the many years that have passed since I served in these positions I will do my best to remember to my best recollection the issues and circumstances involved. Many things have happened to me physically and mentally in these many years and many things I may not be able to remember but I will try my best.

I cannot address and have no knowledge about the program of any kind after the time I left the position several years ago.

In 2005 in order to leverage the National Guard's best source of recruiting assistance, the traditional National Guard Soldier. A process action team (with several states, lawyers, comptrollers, senior Army Guard leaders, National Guard Bureau Joint staff members, Recruiting and Retention Commanders and the Army Strength Division members) was formed to develop the concept and create a detailed Operations Order.

I am very proud of my service in the Army, at all levels and believe that the G-RAP concept was and is one of the most innovative programs ever created dollar for dollar to help military recruiting.

As best I can remember, throughout the phases of the planning and execution, while I was a member of the team, great thought and care was put toward creating an effective and efficient tool to help the Army Guard recruit and retain individuals to fill and deploy the combat units to Iraq, Afghanistan and throughout the world, homeland security missions and support to state missions.

The systems, reporting tools, quality assurance and control methods that were available were used to build an effective program.

Throughout the process the team worked with elements of the various staff organizations to ensure that all elements of the program were appropriately reviewed. The fiscal law attorneys (legal review and authority) the contracting policy office, the contracting acquisition office had the authority for contract acquisition since it was separated from the Army Guard Directorate and was at the joint staff under the Chief, National Guard Bureau. We also worked with the comptroller for funding and distribution and other appropriate Army Guard staff offices. Each element was carefully analyzed and reviewed by those above offices.

During the time associated with the program, I remember that the program was in fact monitored on a routine basis to determine how it could be adjusted and improved for greater effectiveness. We were required to provide weekly and often daily updates of the programs results to the leadership at all levels of the Army Guard; additionally we provided routine updates to the Secretary of the Army, the Army G1 and all other relevant staff offices in the Army. Additionally, we briefed individuals inside of the Office of Secretary of Defense for Personnel and Readiness office. Information on the program was provided for congressional testimony products for both the Army Guard and Army that were used in testimony to the House and Senate. Many press/public related events for senior Army Guard and Army leaders to promote the program on a national level.

The program successfully used peer-to-peer recruiting to bring in a great number of high quality individuals who often tested at higher levels, often had low attrition from their enlistment to shipping to basic training and graduated basic training successfully. Then a great many of these who had been recruited by a current Army Guard member himself or herself became involved to recruit individuals from within their sphere of influence.

After a period of time and the demand on all services to recruit members during a prolonged period of war, the Active Army, the Army Reserve and the Air Guard reviewed the program through their appropriate staffing channels (legal, policy, comptroller, contracting, leadership) and decided to adopt the program as an additional part of their recruiting programs.

To my knowledge and understanding of the unique structure of the Army Strength Division as a part of the Army National Guard Directorate being a US Code Title 10 organization and the state Army Guard commands being in a state status under US Code Title 32 there exist no command, supervisory or authority available to the Army Strength Division to supervise local commanders.

On the government side, speaking just to the members of the military. I believe that a great many techniques, training, fraud prevention steps, what to do if anyone was found to be in violation of any program elements, and other guidance were developed and provided to the states.

Additionally, a comprehensive website was used with instructions and verification tools provided to the state commands. This was done because the requirement to provide oversight of Title 32 Army Guard recruiters was explicitly laid out in law, policy and regulations. That authority was with the state adjutant general.

From the beginning of the program the state commands were expected to specifically provide monthly program updates to state senior leaders, conduct continuous program risk assessment, identify program related risk/fraud and take immediate corrective action, notify state chain of command, and to investigate allegations of fraud and take appropriate corrective actions.

At appropriate opportunities such as briefings, monthly video teleconferences with the state Adjutant Generals, training sessions, state visits or other relevant events we would discuss this program in great detail and reinforce that all available actions, safeguards and reviews should be routinely exercised in order to protect government resources and effectively manage the program.

Furthermore, we stated that when potential wrongdoing was found that it should be handled swiftly following all appropriate legal procedures with the agencies available.

As far as potential wrongdoing on part of subcontractor individuals, I believe we were told that we did not have the ability to talk subcontractors about issues like this. If ever we heard of an isolated report we would ask the contractor what was being done to prevent that action and catch any individual doing anything not in accordance with the contract. We were told that they investigate any and all possible wrongdoing and if not verified to be found cleared would suspend that individual, close their account access and conduct further reviews. Then if they found potential criminal activity they were referred to the Criminal Investigative Division or other appropriate agencies. They also provided us with a quite extensive quality assurance and control plan that detailed how they were working to mitigate potential fraud within the subcontractor population. They stated that because of this rigorous process individuals would be found out and when potential criminal wrongdoing was suspected would coordinate with the Criminal Investigate Division for further investigation.

The best I can remember the facts of the period I do not recall the criminal investigation division providing ASM with reports or recommendations of corrective actions nor updates on the issues they were seeing. If I had known of any alleged widespread issues I would have taken actions within my authority to respond, advised all appropriate senior military leaders and worked with the Joint Staff (legal, contracting), Army Guard staff offices and comptroller with the proper authority to take corrective actions.

To the best of my knowledge and remembrance, the team inside of the Army Strength Division who oversaw the daily G-RAP program for the Army Guard did use government databases for checks and balances that were used to verify that we had received an accession through the program. Additionally, we required that additional time elapse between when the individual was verified in the Army recruiting system of record, called

ARISS, and when they were paid. Payments would not be authorized until the individual had been fully loaded into the Army Guard strength system of record, called SIDPRS. This provided additional time to confirm the enlistment data and systems were correct.

Each subcontractor had to first complete an online training program and take an exam that confirmed that they were fully aware of what fraud was, what the rules were and the parameters that they were expected to operate. They also were briefed on the expectation on their part as a recruiting assistant and had to verify that they understood that and would do those tasks. As a refinement to these measures we later asked that all subcontractors in the program be required to conduct sustainment program retraining, validation of their responsibilities and ethics training before they could load any additional individuals.

Anyone who submitted an individual had to certify that they affirmed that they had personally contacted and discussed the benefits of serving in the Army Guard with that individual. This had to be done every time any name was submitted.

When I left the Army Strength Division I was not aware of any widespread or chronic issues in the G-RAP program.

Response to Audit Report

My name is Mike Jones and this is a supplement to my testimony because I received documents after that testimony was submitted.

The Audit report is flawed in several areas.

Generally speaking, the Audit Report that I reviewed bases its conclusions solely on possibilities. More problematic is that basing definitive conclusions on what "could be" or "may have happened" is puzzling. Such as "anything is possible" approach places the auditor's report into the same category as conspiracy theories.

Without appearing flippant or disrespectful, the auditor's report—if complete and if the entire report—seems illustrative of what I would term "audit error" because of glaring deficiencies. It appears that the auditor may have been influenced improperly not to investigate or discover a totality of facts and circumstances for the simple reason that the auditor never opted to interview me personally. I would never allow my staff when I was working in the federal government to write or make accusations without (1) have a complete and full investigation of both sides; and (2) having at least some fact of consequence to support a conclusion.

Holding my staff accountable is what America expects of me and asking departments that support our mission when they expect to fulfill their support roles is part of everyday life in the military, the government, and the private sector.

Accountability for fulfilling one's duties does not constitute any grounds to raise some vague and unknowable notion of "undue pressure," "command influence," or "command pressure". Unfortunately, the audit report makes those terms meaningless and none of the 74 pages in the report speak to any factual basis that might otherwise inform one of what is mean by these vague terms. There are no methods set out in the report to describe how this happened or exactly what happened to constitute some sort of improper standard of accountability. Even the following quotation from a contract officer to suggest improper pressure is strange: "I don't care, get it done." This *oft-used phrase in the military* was purportedly said by unknown ASM leadership. Seen in isolation, even as intentionally laid out in the report, speaks to no other meaning than that the contracting officer was apparently not fulfilling their duty to support ASM and someone at ASM did not want to hear any more of their excuses. But this is not all.

The report goes on to suggest the absurd proposition that even Congress asserted too much pressure. To conclude, there is nothing improper about ensuring that one's staff follows their duties in a timely manner. There is nothing improper about communicating with other departments who are supporting your mission to determine when they will fulfill their job duties and responsibilities. I appropriately led my command

Strangely, the Audit report forgets to tell us what the 15-6 Investigation against me concluded.

I cannot speak to both of the 15-6 investigations because the second one concerned someone else who was in ASM leadership after me. In terms of the 15-6 investigation, the auditor forgot to note that the Army Inspector General found that allegations against me (i.e., fraud, waste, abuse of position, or misconduct in any contracting process) was found completely and absolutely unsubstantiated at all. Given that I was in the National Guard Bureau and that I did not know whom the Army IG was, the report bears independent credibility. The letter exonerating me is attached.

Claiming that Poor Planning Existed Speaks to Ignorance of What Planning Documents Contain

The audit report fails to specifically describe what was 'poor planning' and it does not account for a need to modify a constantly changing, wartime environment. The auditor's conclusions that ASM leadership needed to be herculean in its ability to plan, if remotely true, would mean that the U.S. government would never have to hire contractors because the U.S. government could always predict what will happen in the economy or in a war and take corrective action. What is apparent is that the auditor appears never to have even glossed over the GRAP program documents such as the Frequently Asked Questions and the other many documents. Had the auditor done so, the auditor would have seen that not only was extensive planning done in advance, *but also the planning required to continuously monitoring the changing environment.*

Incumbent should not be able to win an award and Guard personnel should not have a working relationship with incumbent contractors.

The auditor's objections are here, as with other points in the report are conclusory and do not make any sense in terms of what is meant by "close working" relationship. One could say that a close working relationship is important in a war or peacetime environment in any federal contract. Such a relationship is simply not, without more, improper.

Purported rampant fraud activities of recruiters.

Based on the document that I reviewed, the auditor jumps to the conclusion that fraud exists because, out of 10,901 recruiters associated with the recruitment program, 368 are either "still under investigation" or literally, "adjucated" (guilty or innocent we do not know). Once again, the conclusions drawn by the auditor are unclear and do not support any notion of wide spread anything.

Testimony of Philip Crane

U.S. Senate
Homeland Security and Governmental Affairs
Subcommittee on Financial and Contracting Oversight

February 4, 2014

Good morning Chairman McCaskill, Ranking Member Johnson and Committee Members.

Thank you for allowing me to testify today.

I am Philip Crane, President of Docupak, an integrated marketing company founded in 1998 that provides marketing and production capabilities within a single firm to meet client needs with program management, design, packaging, production, inventory control, warehousing and distribution.

Our company also provides other services, including information technology, print-on-demand and development of promotional materials. Docupak does not sell pre-packaged products, but tailors solutions to address each client's unique requirements.

Today I am here to discuss the support we provided to the National Guard Bureau for their Guard Recruiting Assistance Program (G-RAP).

Since the inception of the G-RAP, Docupak established and informed government program and contracting offices of internal controls used to mitigate fraud, waste, and abuse.

Through these efforts, we identified and reported suspected fraud cases to Army CID for investigation and potential prosecution. While the contract was terminated for convenience in 2012, we have continued to assist Army CID and other government agencies in identifying potentially fraudulent activities. To date, we are aware of approximately 28 convicted Recruiting Assistants (RAs) out of the more than 300,000 who participated in the program.

Since its inception, G-RAP has achieved in excess of 149, 000 total accessions and a 92% ship rate to Basic Combat Training for the Army National Guard.

We have consistently made our program records available for full review and audits. As I mentioned in my letter to the Committee requesting this opportunity to testify, our records and employees remain available to Committee members and staff at their convenience.

Throughout the history of the contract, Ernst & Young was retained to audit and to provide assurance that our company's financial statements were precise, complete and accurate. Those audits included an examination of evidence supporting the amounts and disclosures in the financial statements and an assessment of accounting principles used by the company.

I am grateful that the committee allowed me to testify today. Thank you.

* Please see Attachment A

###

solutions here.

po box 1569 · pelham, al 35124 mailing

100 gilbert drive · alabaster, al 35007 delivery

205.621.3378 phone

205.621.2212 fax

888.291.6004 toll-free

www.docupak.com

January 10, 2014

Mr. Jackson Eaton
Counsel
Subcommittee on Financial and Contracting Oversight
U.S. Senate Homeland Security & Governmental Affairs Committee
432 Hart Senate Office Building
Washington, DC 20510

Mr. Eaton:

The Senate Homeland Security & Governmental Affairs Subcommittee on Financial and Contracting Oversight has scheduled a hearing on the Army Recruiting Assistance Programs for Tuesday, February 4, 2014. It is my understanding that no witnesses have been chosen for the hearing. <u>Please consider allowing me, along with appropriate Docupak staff, to appear as witnesses.</u>

I appreciate the opportunity to speak with committee staff again, and also appreciate your kind offer to discuss this matter on a conference call next Wednesday, January 15, 2014, to answer follow up questions to our in-person briefing presented on November 14, 2013. This matter is of utmost importance to our company, and I will fly to Washington, D.C. next Wednesday to meet with the Committee in person.

In addition, I would like to extend an invitation to you and any other Committee Members and Staff to visit our headquarters, meet with our staff, review all relative documents, financial statements, and anything else that would provide Congress a better understanding of how Army Recruiting Assistance Programs were integrated into the entire recruitment process.

In advance, thank you for your time and consideration.

Respectfully,

Philip Crane
President
Document and Packaging Brokers, Inc.

Testimony of Kay Hensen

U.S. Senate
Homeland Security and Governmental Affairs
Subcommittee on Financial and Contracting Oversight

February 4, 2014

Good morning Chairman McCaskill, Ranking Member Johnson and Committee Members.

I am Kay Hensen, former National Guard Bureau Contracting Officer, and now the Corporate Compliance Officer of Docupak. I would like to take a brief moment to provide some background on my experience directly related to my current position at Docupak, where I am responsible for contract procedures, and ensuring compliance of applicable laws and regulations.

Before my employment with Docupak, I served for 27 years in the Military, attaining the rank of Lt. Colonel. During my tenure in the military I served various duties, including logistics, administration, contracting, contract policy, and supervisory positions. My last duty assignment was as the Supervisory Contracting Officer for the Montana National Guard.

After receiving my post-employment clearance from the Montana National Guard ethics counselor, I accepted a position at Docupak, conducting contract audits, reviewing and updating compliance requirements, and developing corporate policy guides for government purchasing.

I have more than a decade of experience in government procurement, from both a government and corporate perspective. My areas of expertise include Federal Acquisition Regulation (FAR), long-term contractual planning, proposal writing, compliance, negotiations, and budget forecasting. In addition, I have a Level III Certification in Contracting from the Defense Acquisition University.

I received my Bachelor of Science Degree in Sociology from Regents College, and a Masters in Business Administration from Touro University.

Today I am here to discuss my duties as a contracting officer for the National Guard Bureau as well as my current duties as the Docupak Compliance Officer.

Thank you for allowing me to participate in this hearing.

*Please see Attachment A

###

DEPARTMENTS OF THE ARMY AND AIR FORCE

JOINT FORCE HEADQUARTERS - MONTANA
P.O. Box 4789
Ft. Harrison, Montana 59636-4789

JA   23 January 2008

MEMORANDUM FOR LTC Kay Hensen, Supervisory Contract Specialist, JFHQ-MT, P.O. Box 4789, Fort Harrison, MT 59636-4789

SUBJECT: Post Government Employment with Document and Packaging Brokers, Inc.

1. On or about 10 January 2008, you requested an opinion from my office regarding any restrictions which may apply to you concerning post-Government employment with Document and Packaging Brokers, Inc. (DOCUPAK). You indicated that you intend to retire in the very near future and have been offered a position with DOCUPAK soon there after. Based upon the information you submitted to me, and subject to the restrictions detailed below, there is no legal objection to your employment with DOCUPAK.

2. In our 10 January 2008 conversation, you have indicated that your new position would entail an in-depth review of DOCUPAK contract proposals to the Department of Defense, to include the National Guard Bureau. You are expected to provide extensive information on the government procurement process and regulations and assist in educating all parties involved on the contracting process.

3. Since 16 April 2006, you have been stationed at the Joint Forces Headquarters-Montana, and held the position of Supervisory Contract Specialist for the Montana National Guard. Your position at JFHQ-MT did not include any procurement or contracting interaction with DOCUPAK. Prior to being stationed at JFHQ-MT, you were a Contracting Officer for the National Guard Bureau. As a Contracting Officer, you purchased supplies, services and information management requirements for the National Guard. You were responsible for planning, coordinating, preparing and staffing contractual pre-award documents and files, technical research, evaluating bids and proposals, negotiating with contractors, and awarding contracts in support of ARNG customers. You were also responsible for contract management of assigned contracts, which consisted of contract placement and administration to include cost control, performance tracking, payment tracking and reconciliation of funding resources, negotiation of modifications, terminations and contract close-outs.

4. In June 2005, you awarded a contract to DOCUPAK, which had a maximum ceiling amount of $200,000,000. The terms of the contract allowed the contract to run until June 2010, provided that the ceiling amount was not reached before that time. However, the ceiling amount was reached in FY 2007. A few delivery orders remain open, but no new awards can be made. A new and different contract was awarded, by a different contracting officer, in the November/December 2007 time frame.

JA
SUBJECT: Post Government Employment with Document and Packaging Brokers, Inc.

5. According to information that you have provided, during the last twelve months of government service, you have not held any position or made decisions that would subject you to the post-Government restrictions of 41 U.S. Code §423, the Procurement Integrity Act.

   a. **18 USC §207** - Generally. you are subject to the representational restrictions of 18 U.S. Code §207 (Encl.). This code provision prohibits you from "switching sides" and representing companies to the government in certain circumstances, but does not prohibit you from providing behind-the-scenes assistance to companies. The length of the restriction varies as set forth below.

   (1) Title 18 U.S. Code §207 (a)(1) establishes a lifetime representation ban regarding parties and particular matters with which you were personally and substantially involved while a federal employee. You may not make with the intent to influence, any communication to, or appearance before, an employee of the United States on behalf of any other person in a particular matter that involved a specific party in which you participated personally and substantially as an officer, if the United States is a party or has a direct and substantial interest in the matter. The term "particular matter" includes any investigation, application, request for a ruling or determination, rulemaking, contract, controversy, claim, charge, accusation, arrest, or judicial or other proceeding. It is important to distinguish among particular matters. The statute does not apply to a broad category of programs when the specific elements may be treated as severable. As noted, the restriction requires that the matter must have involved a specific party or parties other than the United States at the time of the participation. Additionally, the term "particular matter involving a specific party or parties" is interpreted with regard to this requirement to generally not include policy matters such as legislation, the formulation of general policy, standards or objectives, or other action of general application. See 5 CFR §2637.201(c).

   (2) Title 18 U.S. Code § 207(a)(2) sets out a two-year representational restriction that applies to those matters under your official responsibility during your last year of government service. The two-year ban in your case begins on the day after your retirement date. For the purposes of 18 U.S. Code § 207(a)(2), "official responsibility" is defined as the direct administrative or operating authority, whether intermediate or final, and either exercisable alone or with others, and either personally or through subordinates, to approve, disapprove, or otherwise direct Government action. The term "represent" means to make any communication to or appearance before an employee of the United States with the intent to influence that employee in connection with the same particular matter. The two-year representational restriction will apply if a particular matter was under your official responsibility and was actually pending during your last year of federal employment. In order for the prohibition to apply, the government must have a direct and substantial interest in the matter and at the time of the participation, specific parties other than the government must have been involved. The application and view of the term "particular matter involving a specific party or parties" is the same as described above under §207(a)(1).

   (3) To determine what matters were under your "official responsibility" during your last year of work as a federal employee, we look at the position that you held during that time, in other words, your position at the JFHQ-MT. I am not aware of any person under your

JA
SUBJECT: Post Government Employment with Document and Packaging Brokers, Inc.

supervision being involved personally and substantially with a particular matter involving DOCUPAK during your last year as a federal employee. You should contact this office for further clarification if you determine that you had supervisory responsibility for a person who was personally and substantially involved in a particular matter involving DOCUPAK.

b. This opinion is based on information previously provided. Title 18 U.S. Code §207 is a Federal criminal statute and whether or not the statute applies to certain factual situations falls under the jurisdiction of the Department of Justice, not the National Guard Bureau, Department of the Army, or the Department of Defense. This memorandum is an advisory opinion of an agency ethics official and is not binding on the Department of Justice. Finally, note that issuing this ethics guidance to you does not establish an attorney-client relationship. Any communications or information provided between yourself and this office are not protected by the attorney-client privilege nor are they confidential.

If you need additional legal advice regarding post-Government employment, you may reach me at (406) 324-3325 or contact me via e-mail at beverly.schneider@us.army.mil.

Encl.

BEVERLY G. SCHNEIDER
Maj. JA, MTNG
Ethics Counselor

Hearing: Fraud and Abuse in Army Recruiting Contracts
February 4, 2014
Member: Senator McCaskill
Insert: (Page 27, Line 10)
Witness: Maj. Gen. Quantock
File Name: SHSGACCO-01-001-IFR

(The information follows): Since 2007, the Army Criminal Investigation Command (CID) has examined the recruiting assistance records of 312 senior officers. For purposes of this response, "senior officer" is defined as Lieutenant Colonel through General. This total includes, by rank, the following number of senior officers: Major General (14), Brigadier General (35), Colonel (247), and Lieutenant Colonel (16). As of 8 Mar 2014, 270 of these senior officers have been cleared and 42 are currently under investigation. There are 493 officers in the rank of Lieutenant Colonel who are pending initial assessment by CID.

Of the 42 senior officers currently under investigation by CID, 29 have been titled by CID due to a determination that credible information exists to believe they committed an offense. Of these 29 cases, prosecution has been declined in four cases, and the remaining cases are either still under investigation or are pending prosecutorial decision. The four cases and the reasons provided for declination of prosecution are as follows:

Case #1: Declined by the U.S. Attorney's Office for the Eastern District of California due to the low dollar amount of loss to the government.

Case #2: Declined by the U.S. Attorney's Office for the District of New Jersey. This office did not provide a substantive reason for declination. Rather, it made a blanket statement that it would not prosecute any Recruiting Assistance Program (RAP) investigations.

Case #3: Declined by the U.S. Attorney's Office for the Western District of Virginia, who declined to prosecute or provide a legal opinion regarding probable cause.

Case #4: Declined by the U.S. Attorney's Office for the District of Maryland, who stated they would not prosecute RAP investigations unless the cases involved Recruiting Assistants paying off Recruiters. The Maryland State Attorney's Office also declined this investigation because the company (DOCUPAK) was informed of the fraudulent acts but allowed the payments to proceed.

Insert: (Page 27, Line 25)
Witness: Maj. Gen. Quantock
File Name: SHSGACCO-01-002-IFR

(The information follows): The Army Criminal Investigation Division (CID) has no record that any senior leader has been forced to resign as a result of CID's investigations into fraud associated with the Recruiting Assistance Program (RAP).

Insert: (Page 31, Line 8)
Witness: Maj. Gen. Quantock
File Name: SHSGACCO-01-003-IFR

(The information follows): Generally speaking, jurisdiction under the Uniform Code of Military Justice (UCMJ) is limited to those persons in an active duty status in accordance with Title 10 of the United States Code. The Army does not have jurisdiction over members of the Army National Guard of the United States unless those members were in a Title 10 active duty status when the alleged criminal misconduct took place. In the on-going Army Criminal Investigation Division (CID) investigations, none of the senior officers under review were serving in a Title 10 status at the time the offenses were committed. Therefore, they are not subject to disciplinary action under the UCMJ. See UCMJ Article 2(a)(3). As a result, the most viable alternative for pursuing punitive action is civilian criminal jurisdiction.

Insert: (Page 33, Line 15)
Witness: Maj. Gen. Quantock
File Name: SHSGACCO-01-004-IFR

(The information follows): At this stage in its investigations, the Army Criminal Investigation Division (CID) does not have sufficient evidence to conclude or characterize some states has having significantly or systematically more fraud than any other state. To the extent there are differing levels of fraud committed in the different states, CID does not at this point have sufficient information to conclusively state why this might be the case.

This said, CID has uncovered information potentially indicating that select recruiting and retention officials in California may have encouraged fraudulent activity involving the Guard-Recruiting Assistance Program (G-RAP). During an investigation of a recruiting assistant, CID discovered that California Army National Guard (CA ARNG) Recruiting and Retention Command senior NCOs and officers may have abused Active Duty for Special Work (ADSW) and Active Duty Operational Support (ADOS) funds, along with G-RAP contract funds.

Emails provided by witnesses show that a Sergeant Major directing ARNG NCO leaders to have their recruiters "get everything out of G-RAP that is available." Another email stated, "…. Leaders, it appears that our ADSW/ADOS funding has reached its limit. Help your Recruiting Retention NCO's use the G-RAP program to replace lost ADOS as funding is reduced."

Investigation into these emails, what they indicate, and the scope of possible fraudulent activity involving G-RAP is ongoing. We have not seen any indication that officials in any other states facilitated fraudulent activity.

Insert: (Page 37, Line 6)
Witness: Maj. Gen. Quantock
File Name: SHSGACCO-01-005-IFR

(The information follows): As of February 26, 2014, approximately 43% of the 12,984 recruiting assistants not yet cleared by CID would be subject to the Federal 5-year statute of limitations.

Post-Hearing Questions for the Record
Submitted to Lt. Gen. William Grisoli
From Senator Kelly Ayotte

"Fraud and Abuse in Army Recruiting Contracts"
February 4, 2014

1. At the hearing, I addressed a document provided with retired Lieutenant Colonel Kay Hensen's written testimony reports that, "In June 2005…awarded a contract to Docupak, which had a maximum ceiling amount of $200,000,000. The terms of the contract allowed the contract to run until June 2010, provided that the ceiling amount was not reached before that time. However, the ceiling amount was reached in FY 2007." Can you comment on why the ceiling amount was reached approximately three years prior to the contract's end date?

Answer: The U.S. Army Audit Agency reviewed the two Guard-Recruiting Assistance Program (G-RAP) task orders placed against the June 2005 indefinite-delivery/indefinite-quantity (ID/IQ) contract. The June 2005 ID/IQ contract was awarded for marketing and advertising products and services. The G-RAP requirement was not part of the original ID/IQ contract and not considered when the ceiling was established. The two G-RAP tasks orders, which accounted for over $30 million obligated against the contract, contributed to reaching the contract ceiling prior to June 2010. We found that the National Guard Bureau (NGB) did not provide proper oversight of these two G-RAP task orders relying on the contractor to oversee contract execution. Insufficient oversight of these two task orders may have contributed to NGB personnel not being fully aware of contract execution in relation to the contract ceiling amount. However, through the end of Fiscal Year (FY) 2007, NGB issued an additional 74 task orders against the contract for other marketing and advertising products and services which also contributed to reaching the contract ceiling in 2007. We did not audit the award, execution, or oversight of those additional task orders.

Subcommittee on Financial and Contracting Oversight
Hearing title "Fraud and Abuse in Army Recruiting Contracts"
February 5, 2014
QFR from Senator Kelly Ayotte
To Mr. Bentz

Contract Burn Rate

1. Lieutenant General Grisoli, a document provided with retired Lieutenant Colonel Kay Hensen's written testimony reports that, "In June 2005…awarded a contract to Docupak, which had a maximum ceiling amount of $200,000,000. The terms of the contract allowed the contract to run until June 2010, provided that the ceiling amount was not reached before that time. However, the ceiling amount was reached in FY 2007." Can you comment on why the ceiling amount was reached approximately three years prior to the contract's end date?

    A. Mr. Bentz

Answer: The U.S. Army Audit Agency reviewed the two Guard-Recruiting Assistance Program (G-RAP) task orders placed against the June 2005 indefinite-delivery/indefinite-quantity (ID/IQ) contract. The June 2005 ID/IQ contract was awarded for marketing and advertising products and services. The G-RAP requirement was not part of the original ID/IQ contract and not considered when the ceiling was established. The two G-RAP tasks orders, which accounted for over $30 million obligated against the contract, contributed to reaching the contract ceiling prior to June 2010. We found that the National Guard Bureau (NGB) did not provide proper oversight of these two G-RAP task orders relying on the contractor to oversee contract execution. Insufficient oversight of these two task orders may have contributed to NGB personnel not being fully aware of contract execution in relation to the contract ceiling amount. However, through the end of Fiscal Year (FY) 2007, NGB issued an additional 74 task orders against the contract for other marketing and advertising products and services which also contributed to reaching the contract ceiling in 2007. We did not audit the award, execution, or oversight of those additional task orders.

Army Audit Agency

2. Mr. Bentz, how many auditors work in the Army Audit Agency?

Answer: For Fiscal Year 2014, the Army Audit Agency is authorized a total of 578 personnel positions with 525 of those being professional auditors. However, due to current Headquarters, Department of the Army (HQDA) hiring restrictions, our current on-hand strength is only 511 total personnel, 469 being auditors, and we anticipate additional authorization and on-hand reductions through 2019.

3. Mr. Bentz, how many of the Army auditors are forward deployed to Afghanistan?

Answer: The United States Army Audit Agency has maintained a permanent presence in Southwest Asia (SWA) since May 2005. At the height of operations, our SWA workforce totaled as many as 30-35 auditors continually deployed in the Iraq, Afghanistan, and Kuwait areas of operation. During our time in theater, we have deployed, through rotational assignments, well over 200 individual auditors, and we are proud to say all members of our deployment teams have been volunteers. Our deployed workforce has been made up of Agency auditors volunteering as either "Core" team members (auditors pledging a 1 3 year commitment), or "Augmentee" team members (committing to a 180-day rotation).

In the last 18-20 months, as the Army and coalition forces have continued to draw down in SWA, we have also reduced our auditor workforce in theater. Our reductions have been coordinated with Army leadership, leadership in theater, and key members of the oversight community operating in Afghanistan (to include the Special Inspector General for Afghanistan Reconstruction (SIGAR), the Department of Defense Inspector General (DoDIG), the Defense Criminal Investigative Service (DCIS), the Army Criminal Investigations Division (CID), the International Contract Corruption Task Force, and Task Force 2010) to ensure continued audit coverage of high risk areas and leadership priorities.

Presently, we are in our last deployment of auditors to SWA with a 5 person team of auditors stationed in Kuwait and deploying to Afghanistan as the mission requires.

4. Mr. Bentz, given some of the contract corruption we have seen in contracts in Afghanistan, would it make more sense to have more Army auditors forward deployed looking at Army contracting in Afghanistan?

Answer: Because the operations in SWA are in a joint environment, the Special Inspector General for Afghanistan Reconstruction (SIGAR) and the Department of Defense Inspector General (DoDIG) have primary jurisdiction over audits completed there. The United States Army Audit Agency has operated in this joint environment by partnering with various oversight and investigative agencies to include the SIGAR, DoDIG, the Army Criminal Investigations Division (CID), the International Contract Corruption Task Force, and Task Force 2010. We also ensure sufficiency of oversight coverage by coordinating with these various organizations through the SWA Joint Planning Group. The Army Audit Agency has executed an extensive body of work on strategic, programmatic, logistic, and contracting issues supporting military operations in Iraq, Afghanistan, and Kuwait. Our audit teams in theater have published nearly 200 audit reports for Army leaders addressing some of the most significant theater-wide issues to include; the Commanders Emergency Response Program, contingency contracting operations, the Logistics Civil Augmentation Program (LOGCAP) for Operation Iraqi Freedom (OIF) and

Operation Enduring Freedom (OEF), logistics operations, and financial management operations. Our work has addressed all aspects of the contracting process from requirements definition to contract award, administration, and closeout and has included recommendations to address and correct the root causes of poor and inefficient contracting and oversight practices in theater. We have also previously supported Task Force 2010 by detailing a full-time auditor to that unit.

We also have a Continental United States (CONUS) based team focused specifically on identifying and recommending improvements to contracting operations and oversight Army-wide. This team of approximately 30 auditors works with Army leaders to improve the quality and professional accountability of the contracting workforce and contracting operations Army-wide with emphasis on creating lasting change in the performance and culture of the contracting profession and its personnel. Work completed by this team has addressed the growth of the contracting workforce, timing of when military personnel access into the contracting field, training for those military contracting officers, and reviewing contracting operations and the oversight, quality control and accountability mechanisms in place throughout Army contracting offices and activities.